An Introduction to Islamic Psychology

Religion and Psychology

Editor-in-Chief

Ralph W. Hood, Jr. (*University of Tennessee at Chattanooga, USA*)

Associate Editors

Mohammad Khodayarifard (*University of Tehran, Iran*)
Tomas Lindgren (*Umeå Universitet, Sweden*)
Tatjana Schnell (*Universität Innsbruck, Austria*)
Katarzyna Skrzypińska (*University of Gdańsk, Poland*)
W. Paul Williamson (*Henderson State University, Arkadelphia, USA*)

Volumes published in this Brill Research Perspective are listed at *brill.com/rpsys*

An Introduction to Islamic Psychology

By

Mohammad Khodayarifard
Masud Azarbaijani
Rouhollah Shahabi
Saeid Zandi

BRILL

LEIDEN | BOSTON

Library of Congress Control Number: 2021920482

Typeface for the Latin, Greek, and Cyrillic scripts: "Brill". See and download: brill.com/brill-typeface.

ISSN 2772-2783
ISBN 978-90-04-50574-2 (paperback)
ISBN 978-90-04-50575-9 (e-book)

Copyright 2022 by Mohammad Khodayarifard, Masud Azarbaijani, Rouhollah Shahabi and Saeid Zandi.
Published by Koninklijke Brill NV, Leiden, The Netherlands.
Koninklijke Brill NV incorporates the imprints Brill, Brill Nijhoff, Brill Hotei, Brill Schöningh, Brill Fink, Brill mentis, Vandenhoeck & Ruprecht, Böhlau Verlag and V&R Unipress.
Koninklijke Brill NV reserves the right to protect this publication against unauthorized use. Requests for re-use and/or translations must be addressed to Koninklijke Brill NV via brill.com or copyright.com.

This book is printed on acid-free paper and produced in a sustainable manner.

Contents

Foreword VII

Preface IX

Abstract 1

Keywords 1

1 Possibility, Foundations, and Characteristics of Islamic Psychology 1

  1.1 *Philosophical Foundations of Modern Psychology* 2

  1.2 *Theoretical and Philosophical Challenges of Modern Psychology* 5

  1.3 *What Is the Solution to the Aforementioned Challenges?* 9

  1.4 *Is a Religious or Islamic Psychology Possible?* 9

  1.5 Rūḥ 13

  1.6 Fitrah 14

  1.7 Amal 16

  1.8 Nafs 16

  1.9 *Definition of the Islamic Psychology* 19

  1.10 *Have Islamic Psychology and Western Psychology Been Closer to One Another in the Recent Decade?* 20

  1.11 *Summary* 22

2 Research Methodology in Islamic Psychology 24

  2.1 *Research Paradigms in the Social Sciences* 25

    2.1.1 Positivist Paradigm 25

    2.1.2 Research Methods Based on the Positivist Paradigm 26

    2.1.3 Interpretive Paradigm 26

    2.1.4 Research Methods Based on the Interpretive Paradigm 27

    2.1.5 Critical Paradigm 28

    2.1.6 Research Methods Based on the Critical Paradigm 29

    2.1.7 Pragmatic Paradigm 30

    2.1.8 Research Methods Based on the Pragmatic Paradigm 30

  2.2 *Islamic Paradigm* 31

    2.2.1 Research Methods Based on the Islamic Paradigm 31

  2.3 *Summary* 35

3 Personality 37

  3.1 *Structural Approach to Personality* 38

    3.1.1 Personality as *Shakeleh* 38

    3.1.2 Qur'anic Theory of Personality 40

  3.2 *Trait Approach to Personality* 41

    3.2.1 Trait Theory of Personality from the Islamic Perspective 43

    3.2.2 Classification Patterns of Personality Attributes in the Islamic Sources 43

  3.3 *Summary* 47

4   Mental Disorders and Psychotherapy   48
    4.1   *Definition of Mental Health and Mental Illness*   48
    4.2   *Religious Psychotherapy in the Islamic Tradition*   52
    4.3   *Therapeutic Methods with an Islamic Perspective*   57
        4.3.1   Spiritually Multidimensional Psychotherapy   57
        4.3.2   *Reza* and *Tawakkul*   62
        4.3.3   Islamic Therapy for Grief Intervention   62
        4.3.4   Monotheistic Integrated Therapy   63
        4.3.5   Change in Mental Organization Based on Religious Self-Fulfillment Theory   65
        4.3.6   Islamic Multifaceted Treatment   67
        4.3.7   Cognitive-Behavioral Psychotherapy Program Based on Religious Teachings   67
        4.3.8   Positive Thinking with Emphasis on the Islamic Perspective   69
    4.4   *Summary*   73
    Acknowledgments   74
    References   74

Foreword

All too often, the psychological study of religion is explored by methods that need not take into consideration the differences between religious and scientific worldviews in general or attended to what may be *sui generis* about a specific religion. Mohammad Khodayarifard and his co-authors are competent psychologists of faith who present the case for a new paradigm for the psychology of religion. The paradigm does justice to both scientific and religious worldviews, but most important it presents what is *sui generis* about the new paradigm, Islamic psychology.

Part of the justification for the new paradigm is that modern psychology demands theoretical and methodological exclusion of the transcendent. It confines itself to the constraints of natural science. While experimental methods, operationalization, and measurement serve the physical and other natural sciences well, this scientific positivism is inadequate to a psychology of religion in general and to the Islamic paradigm in particular. Islam has never been opposed to science but neither has it succumbed to a psychology that denies the spiritual nature of individuals nor their creator. Terms as *amal, fitrah, nafs*, and *wahy* cannot be reduced to definitions that exclude transcendence. The inclusion of transcendence demands a dialogue between a psychology open to the transcendent and to ontological realities inherent in religious worldviews. This proposal for an Islamic paradigm takes its ontological claims seriously. It also demonstrates the rich diversity that is possible within this new paradigm.

The absolute *sui generis* truth claim fundamental to the Islamic paradigm is that Qur'anic truth is eternal and unchanging. However, it does not follow from this absolute truth claim that diversity is not possible within this new paradigm. Qur'anic truth must be interpreted and understood. This is a uniquely human act. Factual truths of the natural world have long been accepted in Islam as capable of empirical investigation. One would be foolish not to accept as true the best approximation to reality that science can provide. However, the collective scientific understanding unfolds over time. While Qur'anic truth does not change, our scientific understanding of the scientific truths does as humans advance in their understanding of the created world.

A second point is crucial to a proper understanding of the diversity possible within the proposed new paradigm. Transcendent truths are always open to interpretation. Persons have wide freedom in interpretation and can dialogue and debate differences of sincerely held opinions within the new Islamic paradigm. Since interpreted truths are not absolute, their discussion further justifies reference to the diversity possible within Islamic psychology.

Finally, there exist what can best be described as pragmatic truths. These include instinctive human concerns with ethics, the use of technology, and the economic and political organization – all, which represents lived human existence. These involve truth claims either derived from scientific (factual) or from transcendent truths and thus exhibit great diversity among the faithful in Islam that nevertheless remain unified in terms of one absolute *sui generis* Qur'anic truth.

The authors are respectfully mindful that other paradigms have been proposed based upon different faith traditions such as Buddhism and Christianity. How could we not welcome this call for an Islamic psychology?

Ralph W. Hood Jr

Preface

Contemporary psychology is influenced by scientific naturalism and positivism. Psychological studies attempt to have the best possible control over variables and to have the experiments as close to physical and experimental studies as possible; they provide operational definitions for completely subjective constructs and concepts so as to make them more tangible. They also make use of the most complicated statistical methods and techniques in order to reach the most objective conclusions. Such an attempt is admirable in natural sciences because it has led to a better life, but it cannot be the sole path for sciences related to human nature – especially psychology – to study the mental processes and behavior of human beings. According to Islamic teachings, human beings have an eternal soul, God-seeking *fitrah*,[1] sick/reassured soul and heart, and a life purpose coordinated with the physiological body. What is the place of these concepts in methodology and consequently in present knowledge of contemporary psychology? Regarding the study of human beings' mental processes and behavior, one may ask the question of whether it is basically possible to ignore them all under the pretext that presenting an operational definition of them is not possible or whether it is possible to pay attention to just the parts that can be studied through today's operationalization and experimental method. Such a view limits contemporary psychology to just a supporter of the knowledge gained via experience and deprives it of more qualitative sources of knowledge such as *wahy*.[2] It is clear that today's experimental psychology has discovered and presented numerous aspects of change, cognition, feeling, emotion, and harms with regard to human beings, which are really acceptable, usable, and continuously applicable. However, one must admit that seeing human beings without any look at their Creator, disregarding the ongoing sovereignty of God over human beings after Creation, ignoring *wahy* as a source of knowledge, mere emphasis on experimental and operationalized aspects, and inability to move toward the subjects which have metaphysical assumptions are the most important challenges faced by the experimental psychology. Obviously, the outcome of such a viewpoint is the description of human beings within only the framework of experimental and natural processes. Is such a description really a comprehensive one?

---

1 *Fitrah* refers to the human nature and inner predispositions in the state of perfection and uprightness according to which Allah created it.

2 *Wahy* is the Arabic word for revelation. In Islamic belief, revelations are God's Word delivered by chosen individuals – known as Messenger prophets – to mankind.

The experimental approach to psychology, despite all of the mentioned challenges and limits, has lots of proponents; the bias in favor of positivism has moved so forward that the history of experimental psychology has been presented in an unreal, positive, and illusionary fashion. In an interesting study, Harris (1997) compared the main outcomes of classical psychology studies with that of their rewrites in different books. According to most of the present psychology books, in the study conducted by Watson and Raynor (1920), little Albert's phobia of rabbits developed easily, and he then generalized it to all furry white objects. However, in the main study, Albert's phobia developed difficultly, was temporary, and did not have a significant relationship with color or coverings of objects.

The present book includes four parts. In part one, after that, a general definition of psychology is presented, philosophical foundations and modern psychology challenges are reviewed from an Islamic standpoint. Then, the establishment of a kind of Islamic psychology has been suggested in order to face these challenges. In this regard, the possibility, foundations, and characteristics of Islamic psychology have also been introduced. In part two, after that, the research paradigms in the social sciences are introduced, research methods based on the Islamic paradigm are concisely elaborated. To familiarize readers with basic concepts of psychology from an Islamic perspective, parts 3 and 4 have dealt with personality, mental disorders, and psychotherapy. In part 3, both structural and trait approaches to personality have been taken into consideration from an Islamic perspective. At first, the structure of personality has been discussed through an Islamic framework; then, within a trait approach to personality, positive character traits such as kindness, humbleness, and justice and negative character traits such as arrogance and hypocrisy have been noticed based on Qur'anic sources. In part 4, mental disease and health and also the therapeutic methods related to them are introduced from the perspective of Islam.

In the end, we hope readers find this work informative and useful. All professors, scholars, psychologists, and students are welcome to put forward their comments and suggestions on this book so that we would take them into account in our future works.

An Introduction to Islamic Psychology

Mohammad Khodayarifard,[1] Masud Azarbaijani,[2] Rouhollah Shahabi,[3] Saeid Zandi[4]

[1]Department of Psychology, Faculty of Psychology and Education, University of Tehran, Iran; *khodayar@ut.ac.ir*; [2]Department of Psychology, Behavioral Sciences Research Institute, Research Institute of Hawzeh and University, Tehran, Iran; [3]Department of Psychology, Institute of Humanities and Cultural Studies, Tehran, Iran; [4]Department of Counselling, Faculty of Psychology and Education, Allameh Tabataba'i University, Tehran, Iran

Abstract

Contemporary psychology is highly influenced by positivism and scientific naturalism. Psychological studies make efforts to control the variables and provide operational definitions of subjective constructs in order to reach the most concrete conclusions. Such efforts are admirable in natural sciences since they have led to a better life. But, this worldview has deprived contemporary psychology of more qualitative sources of knowledge like *wahy* (revelation). The present book introduces Islamic psychology as a paradigm, which can apply *wahy* knowledge and consider religious/spiritual dimensions of humans in scientific exploration. The first part discusses the possibility, foundations, and characteristics of Islamic psychology. The second part introduces research methodology in Islamic psychology. The third part reviews the Qur'anic theory of personality and highlights the concept of *shakeleh*. Finally, the fourth part presents the theories and methods of religious psychotherapy in the Islamic tradition. Each part provides introductory content for readers interested in Islamic psychology.

Keywords

cultural psychology – Islam-based psychology – psychology of religion – religious psychology – theistic psychology

1 Possibility, Foundations, and Characteristics of Islamic Psychology

The spread of the philosophical viewpoint of positivism has led to the emergence of a new concept of science. According to this viewpoint, observation

© MOHAMMAD KHODAYARIFARD ET AL., 2022 | DOI:10.1163/9789004505759_002 is the only trustworthy basis and path to acquire knowledge; hence, any scientific activity begins with direct sensorial observation. Then, as observations increase in number, a hypothesis emerges, and when the hypothesis is frequently tested, repeated, and confirmed, the law is formulated. A hypothesis that is sufficiently repeated and confirmed takes real shape and becomes a stable scientific matter. From such a standpoint, scientific experience is considered as something impersonal, tangible, and out of a scientist's mind, and the scientist is seen as a person who only discovers the things which exist outside (Lotfi, 2002). Scientists of experimental natural sciences such as physics and chemistry had no problem in coming under the umbrella of natural sciences, but scientists of some of the social and humanitarian sciences such as psychology who needed to be recognized had no choice other than to adopt or establish a kind of natural human science, so they studied human behavior in the laboratories and followed the positivism philosophy. In this way, modern psychology was founded in 1879 with studying human behavior in a laboratory in Leipzig, Germany.

In December 1879, under the influence of the mentioned background, Wilhelm Wundt (1832–1920) made the first efforts to measure human behavior. He believed that mental processes are measurable and can be studied quantitatively. Based on such a belief, he did an experiment to know about the length of time that the human brain and nervous system need for turning information into action (Santrock, 2018). On the other hand, although it is clear that recognition of psychology as a scientific field has stemmed from applying the methods of the natural sciences to studying human behavior, less attention has been paid to the simultaneous effect of naturalism and studies of Charles Darvin (1809–1882) on such a scientific recognition of psychology. Let us not forget that when psychology came up as a science in the late 19th century, the atmosphere of thinking was heavily influenced by the works of the English naturalist Charles Darvin (Santrock, 2018). Such foundations have critical challenges, which will be discussed later through the following of the aforementioned theoretical background and its challenges.

1.1 *Philosophical Foundations of Modern Psychology*
The theoretical and philosophical background from which psychology emerged within an experimental framework can be obviously observed in the works of some scientists before the year 1879 (the starting point of modern psychology), such as John Locke and David Hume.

John Locke (1632–1704) rejects a rationalistic interpretation of innate concepts (innate concepts of mind whose truth is clear and unquestionable to human); through a mechanical interpretation of the human mind, he believes that it is impossible that the mind possesses a series of pre-existing concepts which determine the framework of individual's later experience, but he sees the human mind as a blank slate or white paper on which experience is imprinted later. According to Locke, there are two kinds of experience: first, the ideas that are rooted in observation of external objects and provide us with a direct, unmediated awareness of the outside world through the five senses, e.g., coldness of ice; second, thinking and reasoning about the senses that have entered the mind. To Locke, a child who has not ever seen any colors except black and white would have no concept of red and green colors; so, on the occasion that the human mind is not stimulated by senses, it would remain inactive and inert (Copleston, 2014; Zibakalam, 2007).

Hume (1711–1776) put more effort into presenting a mechanical interpretation of the human mind. He called all of the contents of the human mind *perceptions*, which he – like Locke – divided into two types: a) impressions, which are immediate data of sense perceptions; b) thoughts or ideas, which are fainted images of impressions, i.e., after that direct relationship of senses is disconnected, a weak fainted image of that object remains inside the mind, and Hume calls this weak fainted image *thought* or *idea* (Copleston, 2014). For example, when a person directly observes a tree, the impression of that tree's visual figure is formed in their eyes, but when the tree is absent, the person has a fainted image of that impression, which is named *thought* or *idea*. Therefore, for Hume, whether an idea is derived from its corresponding impression or it is a mixture of broader ideas which themselves are derived from their corresponding impressions, all perceptions of human being stem directly and indirectly from experience, and it is not possible for a human being to have a perception which is not derived from experience.[1] Such a conclusion involves a secondary conclusion concerning the meaningfulness of words: the meaning of a word is the mental idea of that word, the mental idea emerges through sensory impression, and impression results from experience. Therefore, if there is

---

1 It is worth noting that later positive interpretations of Hume's theory emphasized that the major purpose of Hume was to show how human obtains their fundamental beliefs, which are not attainable through reason and experience, and to show that there is also a third source named nature or instinct. In other words, Hume was aware of the skepticism lied at the heart of positivism and did not aim to expand this skepticism, but his goal was to explain the fact that some of the fundamental beliefs are primitive constructions, which we already have in our minds in accordance with nature; i.e. regarding the fundamental beliefs, Hume proposes a negative phase and a positive phase, but empiricists have paid more attention to his account of the negative phase (Morvarid & Haghi, 2009). This interpretation of Hume's theory has received little attention by scientists. However, it does not deny the effect of negative phase of Hume's theory on categorization of psychology within the framework of positivism.

a word of which no experience exists in the outside world, that word would be considered to be meaningless. Such consideration has had a huge impact on the concepts studied in modern psychology from the beginning until now, so modern psychology avoids the scientific study of anything that is not measurable, i.e., anything that lacks a corresponding experience.

On the other hand, almost all of the historians of psychology confirm the effect of naturalism on the emergence of psychology. Today also, most of the scientists of the behavioral sciences, such as psychology, regard scientific naturalism as their major prerequisite and ground their studies' theories and methodologies on its assumptions. According to this viewpoint, the interpretation of the world acquired via science is the only satisfactory interpretation of reality; this viewpoint – even in its weakest form – supposes that acquiring a comprehensive knowledge about the natural and social world [such as human behavior] does not require to refer to God because the world, without supernatural control or causes, is self-sufficient. Perhaps two of the main features of the naturalistic approach are the following: firstly, interpretation of the objective world without any reference to God (Slife, Mitchel, & Whooly, 2004); secondly, the sovereignty of physical and natural principles and laws over many incidents and processes in the world (Griffin, 2000). The first feature can be regarded as a methodological naturalism that is committed to providing rule-governed interpretations of phenomena without any reference to supernatural forces like God. This method believes that a phenomenon is only recognized through the eyes of an external observer in an objective, impartial way. The second feature can be regarded as a reductionist naturalism trying to present a single interpretation of the human and non-human world by removing the distinction between human and non-human. For instance, it believes that objects fall down just because of the law of attraction or that Mother Nature is the cause of given incidents. In other words, under the belief that there is an assumed rule-governed order, human and non-human have been seen as distinctive pieces of nature which work on the basis of specific stable principles (Numbers, 2003).

Being aware of the problems of this viewpoint, some scholars tried to make a compromise between naturalistic and theistic viewpoints. Some of them believe that God has created the naturalistic order of the world, but this divine creature is no longer under God's ongoing operation and control. It seems that such a claim cannot mean a compromise between naturalistic and theistic viewpoints because this approach believes that God is active at some point of time (at the time of creation), and then the natural and human affairs are designated to the naturalistic world while God is absent and ineffective. Inefficacy of such a view has led to the development of dualism (the existence of both body and mind or soul) among western thinkers and has continued until today. Affected by the two mentioned features, the main movements of psychology have rarely made use of divine to interpret psychological phenomena (first feature), and they test their theoretical principles through physical and natural principles and laws (second feature) (Slife et al., 2004).

In general, such theoretical and philosophical ground has paved the way for presenting psychology as natural science. In this regard, psychology is a science that employs experimental methods to study mental, psychological, and behavioral phenomena scientifically; i.e., first, it makes a hypothesis about a psychological phenomenon, then it tests that hypothesis through reliable methods, in a way that others be also able to repeat that and reach similar results.

1.2 Theoretical and Philosophical Challenges of Modern Psychology

The previous section concisely explained the most important theoretical and philosophical foundations which established modern psychology within an empiricist and secular framework. This framework encompasses critical challenges:

1. Positivist psychology's neglect of the unseen world: under the pretext that whatever is not observable cannot be scientifically studied either, modern psychology has neglected the unseen world. It was because of such standpoint that some of the most significant aspects of human, namely mind, consciousness, ethics, responsibility, meaning-making, purpose, and belief in God, have been underestimated and neglected for years. This issue would be of greater importance at the time of talking about the professions or individuals whose purpose is to help others or to make others develop personally (Richards & Bergin, 2005). It is axiomatic that in the Islamic conceptualization, the reality is much more complicated than that of modern psychology; the unseen world – the phenomena or aspects which are not identified through using the typical powers of human – is really much wider than the observable world, and the *unseen* interacts with and has effects on the observable world.

2. Richards and Bergin (2005) believe that in recent years, [western] psychologists and philosophers have started identifying the limitations of their theoretical foundations. Many of them have a consensus on the fact that "scientific naturalism presents a weak viewpoint on the nature of humans and cannot comprehensively interpret the complexities and ambiguities of the world and life." Griffin (2000) states that when atheism combines sensations and materialism, the output would be a deterministic, relativistic, and nihilistic worldview in which life has no ultimate

meaning. Even behavioral scientists reject scientific naturalism's negative viewpoint on the nature of humans and consider it to be insufficient because they believe that this point of view denies some of the most significant aspects of humans.

3. In modern psychology, humans have been seen as independent from their creator; some of the dominant western psychology schools, such as psychoanalysis and behaviorism, deny the existence of any internal religious tendency in the human psyche or do not venture to talk about this realm (Abu-Raiya, 2012). Under the pretext that the human soul is an invisible, intangible, and spiritual phenomenon and cannot be studied experimentally, major western schools of psychology did not pay much attention to the spiritual nature of human beings. On the contrary, as Hood (in press) mentions,

> recent proposals for a theistic psychology clash most strongly with advocates of psychological science which are largely restricted to an epistemological naturalism. Theistic psychologies transcend epistemological naturalism and introduce non-material ontological considerations into psychology as a possible competing paradigm in which spiritual realities co-exist with the physical and are explicitly acknowledged.

Theistic psychology disagrees not just with psychological science but scientific naturalism. It accepts the reality of transcendent non-material realities (Hood, in press). As Iqbal and Skinner (2021, 65) noted,

> given the importance of religion, the American Psychological Association (APA) has division 36, 'Psychology of religion'. But the perspective of mainstream psychology does not acknowledge the spiritual nature of human beings and their connection to God. Islamic psychology is one of the religion-based perspectives which acknowledges it. This perspective has also attracted the attention of western psychologists.

The Islamic viewpoint, as a ground for Islamic approaches to psychology,[2] believes that humanity is created to worship God and that worshipping

---

2 Kaplick and Skinner (2017) classified the efforts done in the area of Islamic perspective in psychology into the following different trends: 1. The Islamic Filter Approach: This approach was introduced by Badri (1979, 2016). "He criticized Muslim psychologists for accepting Western psychological theories uncritically." (Iqbal & Skinner, 2021, 69). This approach focuses on

God is the main reason behind the creation of human beings.[3] On the other hand, human has a dual nature, including body and soul. The body belongs to the World of Creation, can be subject to transformation, evolution, and change, and is limited to space and time, but the soul belongs to the World of Command, so it is free of space and time and does not fade away after death. Such invisibility cannot justify the lack of study on and attention toward it for psychological interpretation of human behavior. Accordingly, humans must be regarded as a bio-psycho-socio-spiritual (biological, psychological, social, spiritual) being, not as a bio-psychosocial one; this standpoint is now accepted by western schools of psychology too.

4. In recent years, western psychologists are of the opinion that human has a spiritual nature and that human being is a bio-psycho-socio-spiritual creature. Regarding the spiritual perspective of western psychologists, although religion is historically a construct that has wide borders and contains both personal and institutional elements, nowadays the attention is mostly paid to its institutional aspect; on the other hand, spirituality is considered a desirable term to describe personal experiences of matters like personal excellence, paraconscious sensitivity, and meaning-orientedness. However, an Islamic perspective does not accept dividing the religion into institutional and personal aspects and consequently separating the religiosity from spirituality (Khodayarifard et al., 2019; Khodayarifard et al., 2016b), so basically, the concept of spirituality has never been used in resources like Dehkhoda Dictionary, Nafisi Dictionary, and Islamic resources such as Quran and Sunnah[4] of Prophet Mohammad (Mesbah, 2010); likewise, the works of religious scholars

---

critically evaluating the mainstream psychology from an Islamic point of view; however, the Islamic Filter Approach still work within Western psychology tradition. Badri "did not seek to develop a paradigm of Islamic psychology as an alternative to Western psychology" (Iqbal & Skinner, 2021, 69). 2. The Comparison Approach: In this approach, Western psychological concepts are compared with their assumed equivalents in Islamic sources with the aim of finding common ground. 3. Islamic Psychology Approach: Introduced by Skinner (1989), this approach underscores the idea that to develop Islamic psychology, Islamic sources (Qur'anic verses, the prophetic traditions and the works of early Muslim scholars) should be considered as the basis (Iqbal & Skinner, 2021). Here, Islamic psychology is regarded as a novel paradigm.

3 And I (Allah) created not the jinn and human except they should worship Me. (Quran 51:56).

4 Sunnah is the Arabic word for traditional customs and practices; in the Islamic community, it refers to the traditions and practices of the Islamic prophet, Muhammad, that constitute a role model for Muslims to follow. The Sunnah is what all the Muslims of Muhammad's time, evidently saw and followed and passed on to the next generations.

such as Imam Khomeini and Shahid Motahari have rarely made use of the word *spirituality*. Nevertheless, according to Islam, there is a meaningful relationship between the world's outward appearance and the inward world, in a way that the visible world is a manifestation of the inward world and an indication of the meaning hidden in the inward world; so perhaps that's why the creatures of the world are called *ayah*[5] in Quran. According to what just mentioned, Allameh Tabatabaei believes that the spiritual world and spiritual life are based on accepting the principality of the spiritual world, i.e., the world consisted of inner virtues and spiritual status as actual realities outside the reality of the material world and nature (Tabatabaei, 1975, pp 51–52).

5.   Contemporary western psychologists believe that behaviors should not be judged and interpreted as valuable and invaluable. They think that instead of making judgments about goodness and badness or rightness and wrongness of behaviors, psychology should only study and interpret the behaviors. However, within an Islamic viewpoint, to study and interpret some behaviors, the context of rightness and wrongness or appropriateness or inappropriateness of those behaviors should be taken into account. For example, within an Islamic standpoint, the interpretation of "homosexual tendency" or "marital infidelity" should be made in the context of their wrongfulness.

6.   An Islamic viewpoint believes that besides reason and empirical observation of the world, revelation is also one of the main sources of knowledge about all matters, especially human beings. But the, western psychology, under the effect of positivism, ignores revelation as a source of knowledge. Throughout history, human beings have satisfied their thirst for gaining knowledge through using all of the three sources. Although experimental knowledge or natural science has been quantitatively the most important source of knowledge, the knowledge gained through revelation is more qualitative. According to Kasule (2010), there is a close relationship between these three major sources of knowledge, i.e., revelation, reason, and empirical observation. To understand revelation and reach conclusions based on empirical observations, reason is needed. On the other hand, revelation supports reason against mistakes and helps it discover the unseen. Therefore, without revelation, a comprehensive understanding of the human social world would be difficult. So it seems that contemporary western psychologists have not properly made use of revelation as one of the major sources of knowledge and have limited themselves to empirical knowledge. It is admitted that natural science

---

5   In the Qur'anic context, the word means "evidence," "sign," or "miracle."

AN INTRODUCTION TO ISLAMIC PSYCHOLOGY

has the grave problem of being limited to the time dimension; that is, human beings can employ the present existing knowledge to predict the future and interpret the past, but the result would be an uncertain prediction and an unsure interpretation. Nonetheless, until now, a certain prediction of the future and a confident tenable interpretation of the past has only been possible through revelation. The emphasis placed on revelation does not mean that the Islamic viewpoint ignores or underestimates natural science. Empirical observation is regarded as one of the sources of knowledge in Islam.

7. With the development of cognitive psychology in the second half of the 20th century, hopes of studying subjective phenomena were boosted, but the belief that subjective phenomena can be referred to as observable phenomena through operational definition was the reason why positivist psychology still remained dominant. Factors such as proposing testable hypotheses and operationalizable variables, valid and reliable measurements, research methods used by psychologists and overemphasis on experimental and quasi-experimental methods, and teaching the various methods of statistical analysis implemented in the psychology students' curriculum indicate the ongoing dominance of positivism in today's psychology and consequently the continuance of aforementioned weaknesses and challenges (Breen & Darlaston-Jones, 2008).

1.3   *What Is the Solution to the Aforementioned Challenges?*

It seems that the establishment of another psychology is a must to fight off the mentioned challenges. Such psychology should have some features: seeing the human being as a created creature who is in relation with God, has a divine *fitrah*, and is affected by their own internal forces of *fitrah*; believing that knowing about such human being not only needs empirical methods but also making use of the God's words. The foundation of psychology with such features can be examined merely through paying attention to religious texts and sources. Now the main question is that whether or not it is basically possible to have a "religious psychology" as a general concept and an "Islamic psychology" as a more specific term.

1.4   *Is a Religious or Islamic Psychology Possible?*

It seems that one can imagine three kinds of relationships between religion and psychology: A) psychology of religion; according to Paloutzian (1996; cited in Azarbayjani, 2011) psychology of religion is a spectrum that studies religious behaviors, emotions, and beliefs through a psychological viewpoint. In this regard, the objective is to understand the psychological processes which affect religious experiences and behaviors. This spectrum tries to take account of the multiple environmental, personal, and social impacts on religious experience and behaviors and to contemplate on studies and theories which pave the way for revealing the mediating psychological processes in religiosity. In other words, the psychology of religion examines the formation and emergence of religiosity through a psychological standpoint and tries to describe and explain the backgrounds and factors of religiosity, analyze religiosity, assess religiosity, and express the outcomes and effects of religiosity on personal and social life. William James is the most distinguished figure in psychology of religion, though the works of other famous psychologists like Freud, Jung, Piaget, and Wulff have also discussed quiddity and the evolution of religion within a psychological framework. B) psychology and religion; in this regard, while psychology and religion are considered to be separated from each other, simultaneously, they are also regarded as two sources of knowledge that interact with one another, and their interaction is the subject of examination and investigation. Themes like the relationship between religiosity and mental health, self-esteem, happiness, resilience, coping styles, a tendency towards drugs, and other similar things, and the interpretation of this relationship exist in this realm. C) religious psychology; a kind of psychology that is based on the foundations of religious ontology and epistemology. The critical question is whether such kind of psychology is possible or not.

It seems that the possibility of religious psychology can be examined through either a general perspective, namely the possibility of "religious science," or a more specific perspective, namely the possibility of "Islamic psychology." Regarding the possibility of religious science, there are many supporting and opposing viewpoints, but it is not possible to discuss them here. At the moment, accepting the possibility of realization and emergence of such a science is the basis of the present book.

Within a more specific perspective, the following points must be taken into account in order to investigate the possibility of the existence of Islamic psychology:

1) According to Sahin (2013), some assumptions must be necessarily taken into consideration, and the general conclusions should be presented based on them. The most important ones of these assumptions are as follows: A) the basis of the belief in religious knowledge is the assumption that God, as the Creator of the universe and human, possesses the true knowledge, so the religious knowledge is absolute. However, the belief that religious knowledge is absolute just belongs to the believers of one religion. While religious knowledge is valid for the believer of religion, it is invalid for the nonbeliever of that religion. Thus, religious knowledge is absolute but simultaneously relative too. B) having its own features, religious knowledge is different from scientific knowledge because the

subject matter of scientific knowledge includes the facts and events that undergo examination and observation, whereas the phenomena which do not come under examination and observation will be outside of the realm of modern scientific attempts. c) scientific activity is administered based on the principle of objectivity; that is, the scientist should study the facts and events irrespective of his/her own beliefs and value judgment. D) some subjects such as the existence of God and the oneness of God provide the basis of religion, and the absence of each of these subjects affects the whole religious structure, whereas many subjects are not basics of religion, and their absence has no effect on the essence of religion. That Prophet Muhammad (PBUH) has not ever made a speech on self-reliance, self-efficacy, and some other basic concepts of psychology and that the Sunnah of Prophet lacks knowledge on these subjects does not mean that the religion has shortages, so lack of presence of these subjects in the religion does not inflict any harm on religion. E) the difference between religion and the concept of religion must be distinguished. Religion is impossible to contain errors, but the concept of religion may include errors; there is no paradox or contradiction in the religion, whereas concepts of religion may be paradoxical or contradictory to one another. F) there is one Qur'anic truth that never changes, but it can be the source of various understandings and interpretations. However, the fact that whether other truths are one and absolute or multiple and relative depends on the meaning of their subject and can be divided into three types: 1. Factual truths: such truths are stable and unchangeable unless the facts or events related to them change. These truths can be subject to observation, examination, and measurement, be proposed as a theory within a scientific and philosophical perspective, and be regarded as a truth, not as a theory when confirmed. For instance, the Earth's orbit around the Sun is factual truth, and although there may be different theories about it, one has to accept whatever that is confirmed. 2. Transcendental truths: such truths do not show mathematical certainty, so they provide a great space for freedom and diversity of human's thoughts, and they are interpreted freely without constraint. With regard to these truths, even the followers of a given religion may make different interpretations based on the same holy book they have. 3. Pragmatic truths: truths such as applied ethics, economy, and technology, which are either affected by truth knowledge or transcendent knowledge and are also relative.

After reviewing these assumptions and their relation to the possibility of Islamic psychology, one can claim that it is possible to propose an "Islamic psychology," but the first step to realize that is to mark the borders of the Quran's verses (as the source of Islamic prerequisites). Some of the verses of the Quran are in the realm of factual truths and can be subject to empirical methods, whereas some are related to transcendental truths, and different interpreters may have different views on them. Therefore, one can conclude that the study of the part of human behaviors that is related to factual matters can be common between western and Islamic psychology because it is carried out through using empirical methods; but the study of the part of human behaviors that is related to transcendence and is in need of revelation belongs specifically to the realm of Islamic psychology. At the same time, it is necessary to bear in mind that one cannot expect that a clear and delineated knowledge about human beings can be acquired through making use of a religious book because the understandings and interpretations of the book – depending on different people – would be different. So, Islamic psychology is not psychology derived from or in accordance with revelation, but it is psychology based on the thoughts of the persons who have been under the effect of revelational texts, and it is psychology which its credibility and independence are not extracted from Islamic texts, but from the thoughts and interpretations made on the basis of Islamic texts.

2) As mentioned in the section on theoretical and philosophical challenges of modern psychology, it seems that the researcher's thoughts, philosophy, and beliefs can affect the attitude toward choosing the problem of the study and developing the model and hypothesis to solve that problem. In other words, description, prediction, and interpretation of psychological phenomena and the methods employed are affected by the person's value system, and nowadays, this effect can be better seen by applying qualitative research methods. Since the foundations of epistemology and anthropology in Islam are different from that of other religions, Muslim psychologists can study humans based on the theoretical and philosophical foundations of Islam and facilitate the establishment of Islamic psychology.

3) Being aware of the mentioned challenges, other theoretical schools and religions have attempted to develop psychology based on their own principles and foundations. The following list refers to some of them: *The Principles of Buddhist Psychology* by Kalupahana, *Christian Psychology* by James Stalker, *Issues in Psychology, Psychotherapy, and Judaism* by Seymour Hoffman, and *Judaism and Psychology: Meeting Points* by Aaron Rabinwitz (Forqani, Nouri, & Sheikh-Shoaei, 2014).

Now that the possibility of the existence of Islamic psychology is admitted, a question occurs to us: Which concept can be the fundamental and basic concept of Islamic psychology? The Islamic surveys have regarded the *rūḥ*, *nafs*,

AN INTRODUCTION TO ISLAMIC PSYCHOLOGY   13

fitrah, and *amal* as the fundamental concepts of Islamic psychology. These concepts will be concisely discussed in the following so as to elaborate on the main concept of Islamic psychology, i.e., the *nafs*.

1.5   Rūḥ[6]

A review of the verses of Quran that use the word *rūḥ* or its derivations indicates that this word is employed for the following subjects:

a)   Creation of human. This group of verses focuses on the breathing of *rūḥ* into the human body. The following verses are some examples: "So when I have proportioned him and breathed into him of My [created] spirit, then fall down to him in prostration." (Quran 38:72); "Then He proportioned him and breathed into him from His [created] spirit and made for you hearing and vision and hearts; little are you grateful" (Quran 32:9); "And when I have proportioned him and breathed into him of My [created] spirit, then fall down to him in prostration" (Quran 15:29).

b)   The *rūḥ* and the support for the believers. In these verses, the word *rūḥ* is accompanied by other words to depict the following matters: *rūḥ* in support of the believers, "You will not find a people who believe in Allah and the Last Day having affection for those who oppose Allah and His Messenger, even if they were their fathers or their sons or their brothers or their kindred. Those – He has decreed within their hearts faith and supported them with spirit from Him. And We will admit them to gardens beneath which rivers flow, wherein they abide eternally. Allah is pleased with them, and they are pleased with Him – those are the party of Allah. Unquestionably, the party of Allah – they are the successful" (Quran 58:22); inspiration and revelation of *rūḥ* to special servants of God "He sends down the angels, with the inspiration of His command, upon whom He wills of His servants, [telling them], Warn that there is no deity except Me; so fear Me" (Quran 16:2), "[He is] the Exalted above [all] degrees, Owner of the Throne; He places the spirit inspiration of His command upon whom He wills of His servants to warn of the Day of Meeting" (Quran 40:15), "And thus We have revealed to you an spirit inspiration of Our command. You did not know what is the Book or [what is] faith, but We have made it a light by which We guide whom We will of Our servants. And indeed, [O Muhammad], you guide to a straight path" (Quran 42:52); responses to questions about the *rūḥ*, "And they ask you about the Spirit. Say, 'The Spirit belongs to the domain of my Lord; and you were given only little knowledge'." (Quran 17:85); the descent of the *rūḥ* along with

---

6   Usually translated as "spirit."

angles on the Night of Decree, "The angels and the Spirit descend therein by permission of their Lord for every matter" (Quran 97:4); the status of the *rūḥ* on the Day of Judgement and the role of spirit in the afterlife, "The angels and the Spirit will ascend to Him during a Day the extent of which is fifty thousand years" (Quran 70:4), "The Day that the Spirit and the angels will stand in rows, they will not speak except for one whom the Most Merciful permits, and he will say what is correct" (Quran 78:38).

c) The *rūḥ* and the divine revelation. This part includes the verses that refer to the revelation delivered to the servants who benefit from divine providence. "He sends down the angels, with the spirit inspiration of His command, upon whom He wills of His servants, [telling them], 'Warn that there is no deity except Me; so fear Me.'" (Quran 16:2), "[He is] the Exalted above [all] degrees, Owner of the Throne; He places the spirit inspiration of His command upon whom He wills of His servants to warn of the Day of Meeting" (Quran 40:15).

d) The descent of the *rūḥ* on the Night of Decree. This descent is carried out in companion with angles by permission of God in order to realize every matter and effort, "The angels and the Spirit descend therein by permission of their Lord for every matter" (Quran 97:4).

e) The *rūḥ* and the resurrection. The 4th verse of chapter 70 of Quran ("The angels and the Spirit will ascend to Him during a Day the extent of which is fifty thousand years") is about the ascent of the *rūḥ* and the angles on a day that its duration equals with fifty thousands of worldly years. Shaker and Sobhani (2015) interpreted each classification of the mentioned verses and stated that two components, i.e. life and perfection are the outcome of the common shared meaning of *rūḥ* in Quran. This means that *rūḥ* is the major source of human's perfection and life; depending on what a person deserves, the *rūḥ* in companion with the body can achieve more perfection and a new life, in a way that the perfection of the *rūḥ* may lead to the Holy Spirit, pave the way for receiving revelation as the source of personal and social life and perfection, and make it possible to accept the divine command and the footing of angles' descent.

1.6 Fitrah[7]

The belief in God exists instinctively in human beings. This innate instinct is called *fitrah*, and it is generally defined as the pristine nature inside humans, which draws him/her into believing in God and following His directions. *Fitrah* is a human's intuitive insight into pure existence; it is conscious attraction and intentional tendency toward God. In other words, *fitrah* can be regarded

---

7 Usually translated as "innate nature."

AN INTRODUCTION TO ISLAMIC PSYCHOLOGY

as a special way of creation by which the very existence of human beings is shaped, and human life is created. Javadi Amoli (2010) states that *fitrah* has the following characteristics: 1) knowledge, awareness, innate insight, and pragmatic tendencies of human being are not imposed but they are contrived in human's nature. Hence they are different from the acquired knowledge in that the latter is obtained from external sources. Therefore, human knows and desires God and religion. 2) *fitrah* is impossible to be eliminated through pressure and imposition, so it is unchangeable, stable, and steady though it may be weakened. 3) since *fitrah* is merged with the existence of each of the human beings, concocted already in all human beings, and no human being is created without it, it is widespread and general. 4) since the insight and tendency of human beings are regardful of pure existence and absolute perfection, they are of real value, are the criterion of human's transcendence, and draw the distinction between human being and other living creatures.

Referring to God at the time of distress and suffering is one of the most important pieces of evidence of human *fitrah*. Numerous verses of the Quran and the personal experiences of many people confirm this fact. The following is a sample of such verses:

> And when adversity touches man, he calls upon his Lord, turning to Him [alone]; then when He bestows on him a favor from Himself, he forgets Him whom he called upon before, and he attributes to Allah equals to mislead [people] from His way. Say, 'Enjoy your disbelief for a little; indeed, you are of the companions of the Fire'.
>
> Quran 39:8

> And when adversity touches man, he calls upon Us; then when We bestow on him a favor from Us, he says, 'I have only been given it because of [my] knowledge.' Rather, it is a trial, but most of them do not know.
>
> Quran 39:49

> And when We bestow favor upon man, he turns away and distances himself; but when evil touches him, then he is full of extensive supplication.
>
> Quran 41:51

> And when affliction touches man, he calls upon Us, whether lying on his side or sitting or standing; but when We remove from him his affliction, he continues [in disobedience] as if he had never called upon Us to [remove] an affliction that touched him. Thus is made pleasing to the transgressors that which they have been doing.
>
> Quran 10:12

1.7 Amal[8]

Khosravi and Bagheri (2005) regard *amal* as the principal concept in psychology. They hold the opinion that *amal* is so broad that it covers all human beings, whether believer or nonbeliever, whether their *fitrah* is active or inactive. In such conceptualization, *amal* refers to a behavior (observable or unobservable) and can include three levels, i.e., cognitive, emotional, and voluntary; In other words, in order to attribute an *amal* to a human being, it is essential that A) s/he finds a cognitive image or perception of it, B) s/he has a tendency or desire to realize it, and C) his/her will be focused on its realization. These three types of foundations may function in a complex process in the emergence of *amal*, so there are different forms of *amal* in which these three principles can play a role in different ways. In terms of these principles, the following two points are important: First, *amal* is not the same as obvious behavior; it refers to an obvious behavior only in case it conforms to the above three principles. The second point is that if the inner manifestations of man are in a way that is based on the mentioned principles, it should also be considered as an *amal*; that's why faith and disbelief are considered as *amal* since they are based on cognitive (epistemology), emotional (desire) and voluntary (will) principles. This is despite the fact that they may not be manifested in external behaviors (Bagheri & Khosravi, 2006). In addition, other kinds of *amal* in Islamic texts include the following: (1) The *amal* that concerns external and obvious actions: In such cases, verses such as "those who believe and *do good*" are used. (2) Speech as an *amal*: For example, in verses 4 and 5 of Surah Al-Kahf, "and to warn those who claim, 'Allah has offspring.' ... What a terrible claim that comes out of their mouths! They say nothing but lies." Here, lying is an *amal*. (3) Collective or social *amals*: Although *amal* is primarily individual, but when there is a kind of convergence in the three aforementioned principles in a group of people, it can be considered as collective *amal*. An example of this kind of *amal* can be the reference made to the people of Thamud[9] in verse 12 of Surah Ash-Shams, where only one of them tried to chase and kill the camel but God spoke of a pervasive punishment for all of them.

1.8 Nafs[10]

Allameh Tabatabaei looking thoughtfully at the first verse of chapter 4 of the Holy Quran, "fear your Lord, who created you from one soul," believes that

---

8   Usually translated as "action."

9   An Arabian tribe that suffered from the divine punishment after refusing to accept the call of the Prophet Salih.

10   Usually translated as "soul."

nafs means the very essence of everything; *nafs* is something because of which human is human, and it is the sum of the *rūḥ* and the body in the world and the *rūḥ* alone in the limbo (Tabatabaei, 1984, Vol 4:213). In fact, depending on the context, *nafs* is of two meanings: the human soul and the self. The term *soul* has been used to refer to either the spirit or whatever that is related to the body or self. Such a changeable usage of words emphasizes on the inherent link between "spirit" and "self." The *nafs* can be considered as something inside human existence that its quiddity is not precisely obvious and that is ready to accept guidance towards either good or evil. It combines human characteristics with the characteristics which have a clear effect on human behavior. Most of Muslim scientists believe that the terms "*nafs*" and "*rūḥ*" can be used interchangeably. The main distinction is that *nafs* refers to self when it is inside the body and refers to *rūḥ* when it is separated from the body. This may not always be true, but some Qur'anic verses have approved that. As an example for reference to self, in the verse 38 of Surah Al-Muddaththir we read: "Every *nafs* [self] will be detained for what it has done." Also, verse 72 of Surah Al-Baqarah reads: "This is when a *nafs* [self] was killed and you disputed who the killer was, but Allah revealed what you concealed." As an example for reference to *rūḥ*, in the verses 27–30 of Surah Al-Fajr we read: "O tranquil *nafs* [*rūḥ*]! ... Return to your Lord, well pleased ⸢with Him⸣ and well pleasing ⸢to Him⸣ ... So join My servants, and enter My Paradise." Further, verses 4–5 of Surah Al-Infitar reads: "and when the graves spill out, ⸢then⸣ each *nafs* [*rūḥ*] will know what it has sent forth or left behind."

After reviewing a group of comprehensive evidence, Parhizgar (2010) came to the conclusion that "*nafs*" and "*rūḥ*" are two words suggesting the same fact. However, within a logical procedure, some verses and *hadiths*[11] have used the term "*rūḥ*" for the time when the immaterial dimension is separated from the body and the term "*nafs*" for the time when the immaterial dimension accompanies the body. Therefore, some verses and *hadiths* use the word "*nafs*" when discussing the worldly status of a human's non-physical part and use the word "*rūḥ*" when focusing on the extraterrestrial status and standing.

In general, depending on the choices made by a person, *nafs* will be in one of the following three levels or conditions: the inciting *nafs* (*an-nafs al-'ammārah*), the self-accusing *nafs* (*an-nafs al-luwwāmah*), and the nafs at peace (*an-nafs al-muṭma'innah*). This fact does not mean that every person has three different *nafss*, but – as it would be explained in the following – it means that there are different characteristics or conditions which may be

---

11   In Islam, *hadith* (prophetic tradition) refers to what Muslims believe to be a record of the words, actions, and the silent approval of the Islamic prophet Muhammad.

indicative of one *nafs*. 1) The inciting *nafs*: as depicted in the following verse, the inciting *nafs* is the *nafs* which provoke people into badness, "And I do not acquit myself. Indeed, the soul is a persistent enjoiner of evil, except those upon which my Lord has mercy. Indeed, my Lord is Forgiving and Merciful" (Quran 12:53). The inciting *nafs* is the lowest level of the *nafs*, inclines towards the material world, and seeks physical joys and desires. It is under the control of desires and passions. If people let these lower levels control their *nafs*, they would lose feelings of regret for committing sins. 2) The self-accusing *nafs*: it is the self-reproaching or reproachful *nafs* that recognizes bad behaviors; it takes the blame for mistakes and feels regret. The self-accusing *nafs* also reproaches themselves for not exhibiting a greater number of good behaviors. In fact, this *nafs* is a conscience soul and has moral awareness, though it does not need a heavenly spirit because the mental structure of a human being generates the conscience by itself and feels happy after good conduct while regretful for improper actions (Ejei, 2012). Allah says, "And I swear by the reproaching soul [to the certainty of resurrection]" (Quran 75:2). 3) The *nafs* at peace: as the person's honest belief strengthens inside their heart, their tendency toward committing bad and evil doings weakens, and the *nafs* would be completely under the person's control through inclination towards piety. Such a person likes goodness, inclines to engage in good conduct, and hates doing evil deeds. This level of *nafs* is the *nafs* at peace. "[To the righteous it will be said], 'O reassured soul, return to your Lord, well-pleased and pleasing [to Him], and enter among My [righteous] servants, and enter My Paradise.'" (Quran 89:30).

It seems that the inciting *nafs* is the most effective component of the *nafs* though the conflict between this and the self-accusing *nafs* is resolved by the help of the *nafs* at peace; this resolution entails a state of ultimate calmness, which is the highest level of psycho-spiritual evolution and when the soul is liberated from tension, it is reachable by means of controlling the desires and passions.

Many of the scholars who are in favor of Islamic psychology believe that '*nafs*' is the subject of Islamic psychology because it is comprehensive and encompasses other aforementioned characteristics (Ghobari-Bonab et al., 2019). Linguistically, *nafs* means 'self'. Today's psychology sees 'self' as whatever is related to the person's mental experience of himself/herself. Because of such reasons and the interpretations made by the following verses, more precise meaning of the *nafs* would be 'person,' 'personality,' and 'human kind.'

> And the false deities are unable to [give] them help, nor can they help themselves.
>
> Quran 7:192

There has certainly come to you a Messenger from among yourselves. Grievous to him is what you suffer; [he is] concerned over you and to the believers is kind and merciful.

Quran 9:128

However, it seems that not only has the human a psyche or self with the meaning of a psychological entity but also God has used the term *'nafs'* to describe Himself:

Say, 'To whom belongs whatever is in the heavens and earth?' Say, 'To Allah.' He has decreed upon His soul mercy ...

Quran 6:12

Therefore, by breathing His spirit into humans, not only has God created humans and profoundly inserted His essence into humans, but also He has bestowed upon humans some of His own characteristics and traits.

1.9 *Definition of the Islamic Psychology*

In the previous section, the possibility of the existence of Islamic psychology was investigated, and it was approved after the confirmation of some premises. A question arises now: If it is accepted that there is Islamic psychology, what is the definition of Islamic psychology? According to Iqbal and Skinner (2021, 66),

because of the lack of a clear definition of Islamic psychology, some Muslim psychologists prefer to use the term Islam and psychology instead of Islamic psychology. Kaplick and Skinner (2017) differentiated between Islamic psychology (referring to the psychology developed from Islamic sources, i.e., Islam's version of psychology); and Islam and psychology (referring to the broader movement that relates Islam to psychology in general).

Within all of the available books on introductory psychology in a western context, one can find a general definition of psychology: "The scientific study of behavior and mental processes." Behavior is whatever that a person does or whatever action is visible to others. The mental processes are the invisible, internal, and subjective components such as thoughts, beliefs, feelings, perceptions, and so on, which can be deduced from behavior (Myers, 2007).

As a science, psychology attempts to provide answers to questions like the following: Who are we?, What is the basic essence of us?, What is the source of our thoughts, feelings, and behaviors?, How can we change or reform our thoughts, feelings, and behaviors and the like? To answer these questions through research and the help of the scientific method, some attempts, including inquiry, experiment, and difficult analyses, have been made. The purpose mostly is the description, interpretation, prediction, and control of human behavior, mental processes, and emotions. An alternative definition of psychology within an Islamic framework can be provided: "the study of the *nafs* and the mental, emotional, and behavioral processes, which covers both observable and unobservable aspects of these elements." Such description stems from the belief that *nafs* is the main element of life, and human's mental processes, emotions, and behavior are rooted in it. The human psyche is not just psychological, but it is basically spiritual and metaphysical. The *fitrah* and the pact of monotheism are written on each *nafs*, whether the person is Muslim or not. Therefore, the true quiddity of human beings is spiritual, and just as the body needs water and food to survive, so the *nafs* needs spiritual bond with its source and creator. Without such a condition, the *nafs* would be afflicted by anxiety, depression, and disappointment. Many of the people who suffer from mental health problems suffer from a chronic illness related to the *nafs*, not to the mind.

In the Islamic conceptualization of psychology, all observable and unobservable aspects of the world may affect the human being. In general, contemporary psychological theories are focused on the visible world, relationships, media, and things like that. Islamic psychology makes use of the aspects of the invisible world as well to interpret the human quiddity, i.e., it takes account of God with all of His power and also of Satan and Jinn.[12] This fact does not mean the negation of the concept of free will and choice, but it puts this concept into a context (Hamdan, 2011).

1.10 Have Islamic Psychology and Western Psychology Been Closer to One Another in the Recent Decade?

It seems that recent approaches of western psychology, on the one hand, have paid attention to the spiritual quiddity of human and this attention can be obviously seen in the religious and spiritual therapeutic techniques which have entered into psychotherapy and also in the concepts that exist in the positive psychology such as spiritual intelligence, and on the other hand they have deeply believed in human agency rather than a merely mechanical and clean slate viewpoint. Therefore, one can claim that western psychology has become closer to psychology upon which Muslim psychologists agree though western

---

12   Jinn, also Romanized as djinn or Anglicized as genies, are supernatural creatures in early pre-Islamic Arabian and later Islamic mythology and theology.

and Islamic psychology have completely different views on the source of spiritual quiddity and human agency.

Contemporary western psychology draws a distinction between the institutional aspect and the personal aspect of religion and calls the institutional aspect *religiosity* and the personal aspect *spirituality*; however, the non-ideological and non-religious spirituality – in which worship is drastically minimized, and the objective is mainly to release from suffering than to reach God – is not rejected by contemporary western psychology because this psychology regards that as spirituality. Nelson (2009) states clearly that although looking for higher-level values, internal freedom, and making sense of life, i.e., spirituality, are generally related to God, a disbeliever in God can also engage in searching for meaning and spirituality in the western countries. In Islam, on the other hand, the first requisite for reaping the benefits of spirituality and meaningful life is that the person should adjust all of their life's actions in the direction of one goal, which has innate desirability. Islam introduces God as the source and wellspring of existence and all virtues and sees closeness to God as the major goal of the creation of humans. That's why the ultimate goal of human activity and progress and the greatest level of human perfection are at the highest possible point of the steps towards nearness to God. Therefore, getting to know God is the first step towards this meaningful life and the first move towards the person's spiritual life (Mesbah, 2010).

Regarding the root of the agency, there is also a crucial difference between the viewpoint of western psychologists and that of Islamic psychologists. Bandura (2008) believes that a change in the feelings of personal agency requires something beyond awareness of the consequences of actions performed by the person. The child develops the feeling of personal agency when he/she recognizes that something has happened and sees himself/herself as the agent of that happening. Through such perception of oneself as the doer or agent, the perception of agency extends, i.e. it moves from action causality toward personal causality. When the child finds that touching a hot object leads to pain, eating food leads to comfort, and manipulating the entertaining objects leads to joy, he/she intensifies his/her recognition of himself/herself as the agent. Moreover, such agency does not reflect only a personal experience, but there is a social aspect in this process. As the child grows up and acquires language, he/she is addressed by a personal name and treated as a distinct person. When the child is about 18 months old, he/she uses verbal references to refer to himself/herself and verbally expresses his/her agency as distinct from others; therefore, based on personal and social experiences, the child shapes a dynamic representation of himself/herself as a person distinct from others, who is able to create the events, i.e., agency.

On the other hand, within an Islamic perspective, human is a creature affected by a lot of effective forces: knowledge of and internal tendency toward God (*fitrah*), a strong inclination toward whatever that meets the primary and innate needs of human (The inciting *nafs*), the factor involved in differentiating correct from wrong and good from bad (reason), a force for criticizing oneself at the time of inclination toward wrong deeds (The self-accusing *nafs*), a determining force for action and performance (free will), effective social forces (person-*ummah*[13] relationships), and potential and actual limitations and weaknesses which surround human entity. Bagheri (2004) is of the opinion that within a small-scale view, the outcome of the conflicts between these forces and factors is loss of balance and emergence of disruption in the person, while the outcome of these conflicts within a large-scale view is human "action" or agency. This action not only belongs to the person but also builds and shapes his/her identity. He states that agency has the following features: 1. Reasonability (the behavior of the person emerges because of the fact that he/she considers it reasonable). 2. Decision making (the action of the person emerges because of his/her internal will and decision to do that action). 3. Belligerence (the actions of the human are not always caused by rational and logical reasons; however, they are always related to a reason). 4. Self-deception (the person may engage in a behavior which he/she – in a given level – is aware of its baselessness but in another level inclines to do that by ignoring and disregarding the truth). 5. Systematic deviation (human actions are rooted in a kind of necessity and the human does them compulsorily). Based on what just mentioned, it seems that according to Islam, the root of human agency is not the detection of distinction between oneself and others as a result of observing the outcomes of personal actions and effective social factors, but it is the loss of balance caused by contradictions between effective internal forces and external ones.

1.11   *Summary*

– The theoretical and philosophical ground which led to the introduction of psychology within an empiricist framework can be readily observed in the works of some scholars like John Locke and Hume and in the Darwinian naturalism before the year 1879 (the starting point of modern psychology). With a mechanical interpretation of the human mind, John Locke viewed the human mind as a blank slate on which the experience would be imprinted later. He divided the experience into two types: first, the ideas, which provide us with a direct and unmediated awareness of the outside

---

13   *Ummah* is an Arabic word meaning "community."

world through the five senses, e.g., coldness of ice; second, thinking and reasoning about the senses that have entered the mind. Therefore, Locke believes that if the human mind is not stimulated by the senses, it would remain inactive and inert. Hume put more effort into presenting a mechanical interpretation of the human mind. Like John Locke, he classified the contents of the human mind into two categories: a) immediate data of sense perceptions; b) fainted and pale images of unmediated sense perceptions. Based on this fact, all perceptions of human are directly or indirectly rooted in experience. Likewise, on the basis of Darwinian naturalism, the world was interpreted objectively without any reference to God, and it was under the sovereignty of physical and natural principles and laws. Within such an atmosphere, psychology came up as natural science.

- The theoretical and philosophical basis on which modern psychology is founded has some critical challenges. A number of these challenges are referred to in the following: emphasis on the objective and tangible world though the unseen world affects and interacts with the tangible world; the scientific naturalism's insufficient interpretation of complexities and obscurities of the life in today's world; viewing the human as an entity independent from God and Creator; interpretation of the behaviors of human on the basis of drives, reflections, conditioning, and social effects while there are other significant factors for interpreting the human behavior or there are some behaviors that cannot be interpreted on the basis of the mentioned reasons; putting no values on behaviors whereas some behaviors must be interpreted within a context of values; emphasis on empirical observation and reason as the sources of knowledge while revelation as an important source of knowledge is ignored; and an inefficacious methodology.

- It seems that the foundation of a kind of religious psychology is necessary to cope with the aforementioned challenges. The major question is that whether this foundation is possible or not. During the investigations into the possibility of founding a religious or Islamic psychology, some points and assumptions must be taken into account, including the absoluteness and at the same time, the relativity of religious knowledge, the distinction between religious knowledge and scientific knowledge, the distinction between what basically is religion and what is not, and the distinction between religion and interpretation of religion.

- In Islamic investigations, the *rūḥ*, *nafs*, *fitrah*, and *amal* are the basic concepts of Islamic psychology. The critics believe that *rūḥ*, *nafs*, and *fitrah* cannot be the subject of Islamic psychology because *rūḥ* could not be clearly known and recognized in this world, the *nafs* is general and all-inclusive, and the *fitrah* is limited and inactive, but they believe that *amal* can be regarded as the subject or basic concept of Islamic psychology since it is so broad that covers all humans whether believers or nonbelievers and whether their *fitrah* is active or inactive. On the other hand, numerous groups believe that the *nafs* is so broad that it covers all of the other concepts, including the *amal*, and can be a more appropriate subject for Islamic psychology.

2 Research Methodology in Islamic Psychology

The new sciences, either natural science or humanities, are founded on some postulates and assumptions called a paradigm. In other words, in the philosophy of science, every scientific theory has basic ontological, epistemological, axiological, rhetorical, methodological, and anthropological assumptions and premises, and the whole set of these assumptions is referred to as a paradigm (Patton, 2002). Kuhn (1962) conceptualized a paradigm as "a way to summarize researchers' beliefs about their efforts to create knowledge." The paradigms are not comparable, and since there is no metaparadigmic criterion, it is not possible to differentiate the right paradigm from the wrong one; however, paradigms can be replaced, and when a paradigm is able to answer more questions and resolve more problems, it replaces the former paradigm, but this replacement does not mean that there is a criterion for differentiating right from wrong.

Regarding the nature of humanities in general, four main paradigms are taken into account: positivist paradigm, interpretive paradigm, critical paradigm, and pragmatic paradigm. Each one of these paradigms has a different purpose. In the positivist paradigm, the purpose of science is controlling, and prediction and the mechanism of realizing it is structural interpretation. The purpose of research and science in the interpretive paradigm is discovery, and the mechanism of the interpretive paradigm is based on emic perspective. The critical paradigm's purpose is change and emancipation, and its mechanism is disclosure and unveiling of the unscientific matters and superstitions disguised as scientific data (Kafi, 2014). The primary goal of pragmatism is to create practical knowledge that has utility for action for making purposeful difference in practice. Each one of these paradigms has its own unique methodologies. Now a crucial question arises: If Islamic psychology is approved, what would be its methodology? As an answer to this question, one can claim that on the basis of the contents discussed in part 1, the necessity and possibility of Islamic psychology have been already discussed and passed, but in terms of the methodology of Islamic psychology, lots of discussions and criticisms are needed so as to reach a purified methodology in the domain of behavioral sciences from an Islamic perspective. This part tries to review the existing worldviews and

AN INTRODUCTION TO ISLAMIC PSYCHOLOGY

methodologies in the social sciences and also suggest methods based on the Islamic paradigm.

2.1 *Research Paradigms in the Social Sciences*

2.1.1 Positivist Paradigm

Ontologically, positivism believes that the world has order and consists of observable, distinct, and detailed events. The existence of the social world is basically objective, and it is beyond the awareness of humans, which is a subjective being. Thus, acquiring a reliable and credible knowledge of the social sciences is somehow like the natural science which is pursued in the physical world (Iman, 2011). Human beings and society are regarded as parts of nature, and causative and rule-governed order rules over their relationships and affairs. In this paradigm, the universe has order and is consisted of visible events. This order can be shown through the general proposition and the existence of stable relationships between events or phenomena. This approach holds the view that just the observable and tangible things are real and subject to scientific study. Likewise, human activity is understood as an observable behavior that happens in visible and material conditions (Blaikie, 2016).

In positivist epistemology, knowledge is gained through sense experience and experimental and comparative analyses; the general propositions and concepts are concise forms of specific observations. Here the experience means obtaining information and/or coming up with evidence collected through the five human senses. In fact, the main purpose of this paradigm is to discover causative relationships between the phenomena. Whatever cannot be directly observed would not be regarded as credible knowledge or as a part of credible interpretations of the social phenomena. Since the positivist researcher seeks for discovering the causative rules and relationships between the phenomena, interpretation is, in fact, the answer to the "whys and wherefores" of personal behavior and action; therefore, in this paradigm, "finding the cause," i.e., the manipulation conducted by the researcher to make changes so that an event would happen in the future, will be possible. Hence, based on interpretation, the prediction would be feasible. Simply put, it is because of reliable and precise detection of causative relationships that the possibility of control as the goal of positivist researches is provided, and the prediction takes place on the basis of control (Blaikie & Priest, 2017). According to Creswell and David Creswell (2018), in a positivist view,

> research seeks to develop relevant, true statements, ones that can serve to explain the situation of concern or that describe the causal relationships of interest. In quantitative studies, researchers advance the relationship

among variables and pose this in terms of questions or hypotheses.... Being objective is an essential aspect of competent inquiry; researchers must examine methods and conclusions for bias. For example, standard of validity and reliability are important in quantitative research.

In general, the key assumptions of this position are as the following: 1. In terms of ontology, the universe has a causative, congruent, and unidimensional order; 2. In terms of epistemology, the only way to know about things is through experience and test, and whatever that cannot be experienced or tested would be regarded as outside the realm of science; 3. In terms of methodology, science is generated on the condition that the realities are logically separated from values, so scientific propositions should be expressed and represented based on natural patterns and irrespective of personal, ethical, social, and cultural tendencies and values. The various modes of positivism, in spite of being very different, have common shared meta-theoretical foundations: in terms of ontology, they believe in the independence of structures and actions from human's understanding; in terms of epistemology, they adhere to independence of knowledge from mind in the form of true description; and in terms of methodology, they suggest using the statistical and natural science methods in the area of the social sciences and humanities (Tavana, 2014).

2.1.2 Research Methods Based on the Positivist Paradigm

The research method based on the positivism paradigm is the hypothetico-deductive model with a method of measurement and quantification of human behavior in an objective and statistical way (Iman, 2011), i.e. quantitative methods. The most significant instances of these methods are the following:

- Experimental methods
- Survey methods
- Quantitative content analysis
- Non-participant observation

2.1.3 Interpretive Paradigm

Also known as interpretivist/constructivist paradigm, this paradigm aims at understanding "the world of human experience" (Cohen & Manion, 1994, 36). The interpretive approach or constructivism is rooted in the philosophical thoughts of Max Weber and Wilhelm Dilthey. Expressing the distinction between humanities and natural sciences, Dilthey presented a different view on positivism; this view holds that humanities rely on *verstehen* or an understanding of the daily life experiences of people which originates in a specific historical condition and is not a reality outside human perception, but it is inside human's mind and awareness. The reality is socially constructed through interactions between actors and is interpreted by them; here, the viewpoint of the studied individuals is emphasized, not the observer's point of view (Alitaba-Firouzjay, 2016). The interpretive/constructivist investigators rely mostly upon the "participants' views of the situation under investigation" (Creswell, 2003, p. 8). Rather than proceeding from a theory, the interpretivists "generate or inductively develop a theory or pattern of meanings" (Creswell, 2003, p. 9).

Unlike the positivist paradigm, the interpretive ontology does not see reality as exclusively material and external, but it regards it as something internal and mental which is constructed through interactions between people. Epistemologically, this paradigm emphasizes the role of language and interpretation as essentials of knowing the phenomena. Knowing the social world based on our ability to experience the world is in a way that others also experience that. Within such a situation, the reality is created by people through the experience of and interpretation of the experience of the world (Iman, 2011).

The features of the interpretive paradigm can generally be as the following: 1. There are two worlds; the natural world and the human social world. In terms of quiddity, there is a substantive difference between these two worlds: the natural world consists of objective phenomena while the social world consists of subjective ones; 2. Knowing about the natural world is different from that of the human social world. To know the natural world, the explanation method is used, while the interpretive method is used to discover and know the human social world. The purpose of explanation is to discover the general rules of natural phenomena, and the purpose of interpretation is to discover the hidden meanings of human social phenomena. It is worth noting that knowing the world in an ultimate and comprehensive way is not possible because any knowledge of the world is intertwined with the verbal and subjective framework, so knowledge of the world is always relative and open-ended (Tavana, 2014).

2.1.4   Research Methods Based on the Interpretive Paradigm

In terms of method, the hypothetico-deductive model cannot be employed because the social reality does not wait to be discovered; therefore, the best method for interpreting the reality is to limit it to a specific time and place. Likewise, it is not possible to express the social world experimentally because observable phenomena are simple productions of human interpretation and meaning. This paradigm emphasizes the qualitative methods; the qualitative methods in humanities are mostly anti-positivism and founded on philosophical "phenomenology" and "individualism." According to Flick et al. (2004, 3), qualitative research claims to describe life-worlds 'from the inside out', from the point of view of the people who participate. By so doing it seeks to contribute to a better understanding of social realities and to draw attention to processes, meaning patterns and structural features. Those remain closed to non-participants, but are also, as a rule, not consciously known by actors caught up in their unquestioned daily routine. Qualitative research, with its precise and 'thick' descriptions, does not simply depict reality, nor does it practice exoticism for its own sake. It rather makes use of the unusual or the deviant and unexpected as a source of insight and a mirror whose reflection makes the unknown perceptible in the known, and the known perceptible in the unknown, thereby opening up further possibilities for (self-) recognition.

Based on this paradigm, science has an inductive method and – unlike the beliefs of positivists – is not acquired only through senses and is not void of values (Iman, 2011). Interpretivism claims that quantitative and positivist approaches ignore a significant part of human experience. Interpretivists are of the belief that culture differentiates human from natural phenomena, so the study on human cannot be based on the models of natural science which are developed for knowing about physical phenomena (Hasani, 2010).

The most significant research methods based on this paradigm are the following:

– Grounded theory
– Qualitative content analysis
– Phenomenology
– Ethnography

2.1.5 Critical Paradigm[14]

This paradigm intends to follow the positive points and advantages of the other two paradigms, i.e., positivism and interpretivism, and to obviate the negative points of these paradigms. For instance, although critical paradigm – unlike positivism and like interpretivism – sees the social world as distinct from the natural world, it – like the positivism – does not negate the observation and predetermined rule-governance of the social system. However, proponents of critical paradigm use these points to make changes. As Creswell and David Creswell (2018, 47) well explain,

---

14 Also known as transformative/emancipatory paradigm and advocacy/participatory paradigm.

A transformative worldview holds that research inquiry needs to be intertwined with politics and a political change agenda to confront social oppression at whatever levels it occurs (Mertens, 2010). Thus, the research contains an action agenda for reform that may change lives of the participants, the institutions in which individuals work or live, and the researcher's life. Moreover, specific issues need to be addressed that speak to important social issues of the day, issues such as empowerment, inequality, oppression, domination, suppression, and alienation.... This research also assumes that the inquirer will proceed collaboratively so as to not further marginalize the participants as a result of the inquiry. In this sense, the participants may help design questions, collect data, analyze information, or reap the rewards of the research. Transformative research provides a voice for these participants, raising their consciousness or advancing an agenda for change to improve their lives. It becomes a united voice for reform and change.

Generally, the critical paradigm neither avoids the experimental methods of the positivists nor sees itself free of the need to utilize interpretivism methods for the discovery of meaning. On the one hand, the proponents of critical paradigm – the same as positivists – believe that an empirical level surrounds our experiences, but at the same time, they, unlike positivists, believe that there are also other levels of existence, On the other hand, like interpretivists, they hold the view that unilateral emphasis on scientific objectivity and trying to make human qualities quantifiable lead to ignorance of the meaning of human behavior (Bascar, 2010, cited in Tavana, 2014).

2.1.6 Research Methods Based on the Critical Paradigm

This paradigm holds the view that although measurement and quantification of human behavior are feasible, they are not appropriate and desirable. The major purpose should be to investigate hidden mechanisms which create observable phenomena (for example, means of production is the key mechanism generating social class); in the other words, the ultimate goal of research based on critical paradigm is to measure and verify the underlying structures of reality. This approach considers personal impartiality and objectivity to be important, but it believes that it is impossible not to be affected by the values or to be empty of values. In general, this paradigm emphasizes the development of theoretical knowledge and believes that although empirical data can be helpful throughout this path, it alone would not suffice because the empirical data only presents pieces of evidence of that hidden structure. The main methods based on this paradigm are the following:

- Action research
- Critical discourse analysis
- Critical ethnography
- Qualitative, quantitative or mixed methods[15]

2.1.7 Pragmatic Paradigm

The aim of pragmatism paradigm is to find the shortcomings in the study and to fortify the research by using mixed methodology approach. Instead of method being important, the problem is most salient and researchers are recommended to use all qualitative and quantitative approaches, methods, and techniques in their inquiry to better understand and resolve the problem (Tashakkori & Teddlie, 1998). The main concern is with applications – what works – and solutions to problems (Patton, 1990). As stated in Creswell and David Creswell (2018, 48), the key features of the pragmatic worldview are as follows:

> Pragmatism is not committed to any one system of philosophy and reality. This applies to mixed methods research in that inquirers draw liberally from both quantitative and qualitative assumptions when they engage in their research.... Pragmatists do not see the world as an absolute unity. In a similar way, mixed methods researchers look to many approaches for collecting and analyzing data rather than subscribing to only one way (e.g., quantitative or qualitative). Truth is what works at the time. It is not based in a duality between reality independent of the mind or within the mind.... Mixed methods researchers need to establish a purpose for their mixing, a rationale for the reasons why quantitative and qualitative data need to be mixed in the first place.... Pragmatists have believed in an external world independent of the mind as well as that lodged in the mind. But they believe that we need to stop asking questions about reality and the laws of nature.

2.1.8 Research Methods Based on the Pragmatic Paradigm

In this paradigm, methodology involves combining or integration of qualitative and quantitative research and data in a study. According to Creswell and David Creswell (2018, 51),

---

15 Using these methods, the researcher should be aware of the underlying contextual, historical and political factors inherent to the subject under interrogation (Mertens, 2008).

AN INTRODUCTION TO ISLAMIC PSYCHOLOGY
31

Early thoughts about the value of multiple methods – called mixed methods – resided in the idea that all methods had bias and weaknesses, and the collection of both quantitative and qualitative data neutralized the weaknesses of each form of data.

The major types of mixed methods research designs based on this paradigm are the following:
- Convergent mixed methods
- Explanatory sequential mixed methods
- Exploratory sequential mixed methods

2.2   *Islamic Paradigm*

Kafi (2014), based on the logic of operational definition, presented a model for Islamic sciences which can be taken into consideration. This model is of two dimensions: one dimension is related to taking a stand on the world and humans, while the other dimension discusses epistemology and methodology, which will be reviewed in the following.

2.2.1   Research Methods Based on the Islamic Paradigm

It is worth noting that epistemologically and methodologically, research methodology in theistic science generally differs in some crucial aspects from that of the mainstream science: 1. The philosophical grounds on which the methodology of mainstream science is founded are different from that of theistic science. As it was thoroughly discussed in part one, the methodology of the mainstream science is based on humanism, liberalism, and rationalism, which is clearly different from the Islamic viewpoint in that philosophy is not the foundation of Islamic thought; in the Islamic perspective, which holds that the divine tradition is an unchangeable tradition, philosophy has a mediating role in the relationship between the level of worldview and reality and should be verified by metaphysical levels of worldview and divine tradition. Therefore, there is a need to reach a consensus on anthropology, ontology, and epistemology within an Islamic perspective for a specific scientific field. For instance, what are the features of anthropology appropriate to the science of economics? 2. In terms of theoretical and operational definitions of variables, religious science is radically different from mainstream science. In mainstream science, definitions of variables are based on observable action, but the variables in religious science are determined on the basis of action, insight, and orientation. In other words, in religious science, the concept of behavior or action – only visible behavior – is not subject to sense and experience, so – following the action – the insight must strengthen the action, and the orientation must strengthen the insight. 3. Another difference between the methodology of religious science and the methodology of mainstream science is the effect of the researcher's worldview on the development of a hypothesis. In mainstream science, the researcher is supposed to develop his/her hypothesis without taking personal opinions into account, whereas religious science does not make such claims and believes that the phenomena cannot be observed without a theoretical framework for the whole Creation. 4. The criterion based on which hypothesis is confirmed is another difference between mainstream and religious science. While the empirical method is the only methodology of mainstream science, religious science considers criteria of confirmation to be much broader than the empirical method, so in addition to empirical confirmation, it also takes account of propositions, efficacy, having *sharia*-based proof and finalism. In addition, there is no principality of reality in religious science, but there is a principality of divine unchangeable traditions. 5. Religious science and mainstream science also differ in their views on phenomena. Although both religious and mainstream sciences are interested in studying the reality of the universe at an objective experience level, the mainstream science holds the view that the real world is only physical and that the real world is this world after which no other world exists, whereas the religious science considers the concept of reality and reality of objects to be in a linear hierarchy (Taghavi, 2017). Another significant point is that, unlike the mainstream scientific method, the paradigm of Islamic humanities assumes that values are present at and affect the stages of problem-finding, selecting the evaluation method, and determining the strategies and guidelines.

In terms of the purpose of science, the Islamic paradigm is strikingly different from the other aforementioned paradigms. The purpose of science in the Islamic paradigm is not exclusive to explanation, understanding, or change (according to discussions about the aforementioned paradigms), but – based on Islamic epistemology and within a pluralist approach – the research methods in Islamic psychology include the following:

The empirical method: This has been taken into consideration as one of the sources of knowledge in Islam. Iqbal and Skinner (2021, 72–73) argue that

> we might need to conduct experiments to study some problems. For example, the experiments may be conducted to investigate the effect of prayer, fast, recitation of the scripture, and other rituals on physiological measures such as brain wave, activation of certain brain regions, galvanic skin response (GSR), and blood pressure…. [Additionally,] the phenomenological approach is relevant for studying subjective experiences related to prayer, fast, and recitation of the scripture. Another example is

AN INTRODUCTION TO ISLAMIC PSYCHOLOGY 33

the hermeneutics approach which can be used for interpretation of the scripture.

The Holy Quran has put a heavy emphasis on evidence-based knowledge and has challenged the unobservable claims:

> And they say, 'None will enter Paradise except one who is a Jew or a Christian.' That is [merely] their wishful thinking, Say, 'Produce your proof, if you should be truthful'.
>
> Quran 2:111

The story of Prophet Abraham is a significant example of the importance of empirical observation in Islam. The reason why Prophet Abraham asked God to show him how the dead resuscitate was not that he had weak faith, but because he, as a human, wanted to know and understand. Therefore, Islamic psychology utilizes numerous types of empirical studies' methods – in the same way as methods based on the positivism paradigm – for various basic and practical issues. When positivist research methods are used in Islamic psychology, the important point is the operational definitions of the studied concepts. Therefore, behavioral expressions or markers of a religious concept such as "piety" can be identified by making use of Islamic sources. Then, based on these markers, a valid and reliable measure for measuring that concept is needed so as to undertake an empirical study – through using these instruments – on many religious concepts together with one another or along with common concepts in psychology (Forqani et al., 2014). On the other hand, on the basis of the verses in which divine traditions are mentioned, one can believe in the existence of rules and take action to interpret human phenomena based on those rules.

The study of Khodayarifard et al. (2019) entitled "Religiosity interactional program for university students: Development and validation" can be considered as an example of empirical research in the study of Islamic psychology. In this study, the effectiveness of an indirect religious education program on promoting students' religiosity was investigated empirically. Another research conducted by Khodayarifard et al. (2016b) also utilized the same design.

Methodology of revealed knowledge: with a focus on reliable religious texts, this method tries to know human characteristics. In other words, by making use of revelational data, this method reaches the information which has created the human being with all of his/her complexity and subtleties and knows humans more than anyone else. Put differently, this method identifies and examines some of the general or specific facts that cannot be recognized through empirical methods. Among the studies that have been done using this method, we can mention Kaviani's study (2019) who investigated psychological concepts like motivation, growth and mental health based on the verses of the Holy Quran.

Ijtihad[16] *method*: The *ijtihad* method took shape in the 14th century AH in a systematic way, and its development has continued until now. This method is problem-focused; whenever Muslims faced a problem, they introduced that problem to a *Mujtahid*[17] and asked him to express, on the basis of the Quran and Sunnah, Islam's view on that. The proponents of Islamic science are of the belief that this method can be extended and developed in a way that it can be used for discovering the knowledge of psychology through making use of the rules of *ijtihad*. However, a crucial question arises here: given that – in *fiqh*[18] – *ijtihad* is practiced on the basis of Quran and Sunnah, what are the sources of this method in case it is used for Islamic sciences such as psychology? The answer might be that in addition to the non-confessional approaches – such as reason and experience – which were already discussed, the confessional approach sources such as religious texts, Sunnah, and *ijma*[19] can also be used. Considering the works of Manteghi (2018), the *ijtihad* method can be utilized in 10 steps for studies related to Islamic psychology: 1. Research problem: all research problems in psychology are subject to investigation via utilization of *ijtihad* method. 2. Reviewing the theoretical foundations: after that, the research problem is presented, the researcher can refer to scientific studies and documents and also to religious sources and findings of Islamic scholars to examine the literature of the subject matter of the study. 3. Examination of the rational and philosophical assumptions of the subject matter. 4. Research through non-confessional approach methods: at this stage, the research problem is scrutinized through making use of rational and empirical methods and attempts are made to provide an appropriate answer to the research question. 5. Research by confessional approach methods: in non-confessional approach and confessional approach methods, the investigation can be conducted either simultaneously or one after another. However, the religious texts and Sunnah can be studied to find proper answers, because reaching answers to questions may be possible in this way. 6. Elementary ideation for answers to questions: whether there is an appropriate answer within confessional approach methods or not, it is possible at this stage to reach a conclusion – on the basis of the

---

16   Independent reasoning or the thorough exertion of a jurist's mental faculty in finding a solution to a legal question.

17   An individual who is qualified to exercise *ijtihad* in the evaluation of Islamic law.

18   The body of Islamic law extracted from detailed Islamic sources.

19   The consensus or agreement of Islamic scholars on a point of Islamic law.

AN INTRODUCTION TO ISLAMIC PSYCHOLOGY

whole research – via confessional and non-confessional approaches methods and present the answer in the form of an idea or suggestion. 7. Testing: the extracted idea is tested at this stage. 8. Making adjustments: the feedback given about the idea is collected, and necessary adjustments are made to that. 9. Final answer to a research question: the final answer and attributing it to Islam must be undertaken with meticulous attention to the procedure and content of the research. Testing of the elementary idea might be repeated a few times to ensure that it is appropriate.

In a study by Azarbayjani and Shojaei (2019), dimensions of human, meaning of life, growth in lifespan, mental health, family, behavior and social interaction have been studied using this research method.

Rational or reason-based methods: In an Islamic framework, Khosropanah (2012) sees the rational method as a part of the Hikmi-Ijtihadi model, which is a model based on network realism. He believes that the meaning of network realism is that humans can find out about external realities with the help of concepts, and no concept can thoroughly represent the external reality, but the concepts act as a window through which the realm of reality is reported. The network realism also means that reason starts with primary axioms, which are innately discovered, then arrives at secondary axioms, and afterward – via secondary axioms – reaches some epistemological non-axiomatic and true propositions.

The important point is that the emphasis on employing the rational method in religious science does not mean that the annulled method of rationalist philosophers – in which the analysis of empirical phenomena was carried out only through subjective reasons while objective realities were ignored – would be revived in the religious science, but it means that the rational method would be used only in the cases which their validity is confirmed, and the most obvious of these cases are the metaphysical dimensions and the mathematical and statistical problems of religious science (Bostan et al., 2018). In addition, the following points can be considered as validity criteria for the rational methods: 1) analysis of concepts; 2) criticism of hypotheses before scientific experience as not being irrational and having a minimum of rationality; 3) critical examination of the arguments of proponents and opponents of an idea or theory.

Azarbayjani's study (2020) entitled "Philosophy of Psychology" can be considered as an example of a rational method. In this study, the subject matter of psychology has been analyzed, and subjected to rational critique.

2.3 *Summary*

– The positivism paradigm believes that the social world consists of observable, distinct, and detailed events. This approach holds the view that just the observable and tangible things are real and subject to scientific study.

Human activity is also understood as an observable behavior that happens in visible and material conditions. The research method based on the positivism paradigm is the hypothetico-deductive model with a method of measurement and quantification of human behavior in an objective and statistical way, i.e., quantitative methods. The most significant instances of these methods are the following:
– Experimental methods
– Survey methods
– Quantitative content analysis
– Non-participant observation
– There are two worlds in the interpretive paradigm: the natural world and the human social world. The two worlds differ in nature from one another: the natural world consists of objective phenomena while the social world consists of subjective ones. Knowing about the natural world is different from that of the human social world. To know the natural world, the explanation method is used, while the interpretive method is used to know the human social world. The purpose of explanation is to discover the general rules of natural phenomena, and the purpose of interpretation is to discover the hidden meanings of social/human phenomena. It is worth noting that knowing the world in an ultimate and comprehensive way is not possible because any knowledge of the world is intertwined with the verbal and subjective framework, so knowledge of the world is always relative and open-ended. The most significant research methods based on this paradigm are the following:
– Grounded theory
– Qualitative content analysis
– Phenomenology
– Ethnography
– The critical paradigm believes that the existence not only has an empirical level but also includes a real level that involves the events and phenomena and a deeper level on which the base of the real phenomena is founded, irrespective of whether those phenomena are observable and testable or not. On the other hand, like interpretivism, they hold the view that unilateral emphasis on scientific objectivity and trying to make human qualities quantitative lead to ignorance of the meaning of human behavior. The main methods based on this paradigm are the following:
– Action research
– Critical discourse analysis
– Critical ethnography
– Qualitative, quantitative or mixed methods

AN INTRODUCTION TO ISLAMIC PSYCHOLOGY 37

- The aim of pragmatism paradigm is to find the weaknesses in the study and to strengthen the research by using mixed methodology approach. Instead of method being important, the problem is of the most importance, and the inquirers are recommended to make use of all qualitative and quantitative approaches, methods, and techniques in their inquiry to better understand and solve the problem. The primary mixed methods designs based on this paradigm are the following:
  - Convergent mixed methods
  - Explanatory sequential mixed methods
  - Exploratory sequential mixed methods
- In terms of the purpose of science, the Islamic paradigm is strikingly different from the other aforementioned paradigms. The purpose of science in the Islamic paradigm is not exclusive to explanation, understanding, or change (according to discussions about the aforementioned paradigms), but – based on Islamic epistemology and within a pluralist approach – the research methods in Islamic psychology include the following:
  - Empirical method
  - Methodology of revealed knowledge
  - *Ijtihad* method
  - Rational or reason-based method

3   Personality

Personality is generally defined as consistent patterns of perceiving, relating to, and thinking about the person's environment. We often react to the world and our surroundings in a unique and similar way. Just as human beings differ in physical characteristics, so do they have unique personalities. Depending on different and various views on quiddity of human, different and various theories on personality exist. Free will or determinism, nature or nurture, past or present, uniqueness or generality, balance or progress, and optimism or pessimism over the quiddity of human are the themes that affect the personality theorists' viewpoint at the time of developing their own theories.

Some western psychology approaches to personality will be reviewed here. Freud's psychoanalysis believes that unconscious processes activate the mental structures of thoughts (id, ego, superego), which are permanently in conflict and lay the foundation of personality. Neo-Freudians, the most distinguished figures of whom are Adler, Jung, and Horney, believe that conscious social, interpersonal, and personal factors are important forces in shaping the personality. Humanists such as Rogers and Maslow believe that humans are good in nature and try to achieve self-actualization and utmost personal change. On the other hand, behaviorists like Skinner and Watson saw personality as the observable outcome of reinforcement. Cognitivists like Bandura propose that personality is the result of mutual interaction between learning and internal thinking styles. In the biological approach, psychologists like Sheldon and Wilson are of the belief that genes, hormones, and neurochemicals in the brain have a greater role in regulating the human personality. In the trait approach, the difference between human beings is reduced to a few distinctive behavior styles or traits. In a study on which culture was very important, Hofstede and Hofstede (2005) classified cultural differences between various countries according to five pillars, also called dimensions. These pillars included individualism/collectivism (the importance of individual or the importance of the group), masculinity/femininity (distinctions and overlaps between the roles of men and women), uncertainty avoidance (lowering anxiety by reducing the possibility of certainty), power distance index (the extent that less powerful people accept the unequal distribution of power), short-term or long-term orientation (giving importance to future, past, or present). The results showed that the scores of the Muslim countries that participated in the study, including Malaysia, Indonesia, Bangladesh, Iraq, and Saudi Arabia, were very similar to one another, but when these countries were compared to western countries, the scores were significantly different. According to such studies, the citizens of Muslim countries share similar cultural values which are significantly different from western countries, so such different cultural values or orientations necessitate the development of a model or theory of personality based on Islamic teachings and human nature in Islam.

An Islamic standpoint seems to view personality in two ways: on the one hand, given the quiddity and nature of human in Islam, a structural view on personality – like the view of Freud – can be held; On the other hand, the personality traits of human can be stated based on quiddity of human and Islamic teachings and commands. The first view, i.e., structural view on personality, has a long history among Muslim scientists and will be presented here, mentioning the theory of personality as "*Shakeleh*" (Ahmadi, 2014) and Qur'anic theory of personality (Abu-Raiya, 2012). The second view will be presented via a model designed by Shojaei et al. (2014) using the trait approach.

3.1 Structural Approach to Personality
3.1.1 Personality as Shakeleh
Ahmadi (2014), referring to the 84th verse of chapter 17 of Quran, "Say, 'Each works according to his *Shakeleh*, but your Lord is most knowing of who is best guided in way'.", considers *shakeleh* to be equal with the concept of human

AN INTRODUCTION TO ISLAMIC PSYCHOLOGY 39

personality and tries to interpret this concept so as to interpret the concept of personality within an Islamic view. To him, *shakeleh* has been used in different meanings, including intentions, mood, needs and requirements, religious school of thought, path, and human psychological structure:

1. Intention represents a heartily forethought and commitment to carrying out an action, and it should not be considered to be the same as mere imagination because the forethought to do an action is not possible only through imagination or fantasy, but the intentions are the product of psychological structures or spiritual states, and many of their components are outside the realm of human imagination and thought. Correction or change of this structure is realized through harsh austerities, extremely precise and correct thoughts, and also a huge amount of endeavor and effort.

2. Mood represents a set of mental traits of human which usually emerge out of the person's relationships with people and objects. Mood is the product of heredity and environment, and it is affected by a third factor, i.e., "free will."

3. Requests and needs can be classified into two general categories: physiological needs and psychological needs. Although physiological needs are not learnable, the way of satisfying and facing them is learnable and completely depends on the human psychological structure and mental state. In terms of psychological needs, some of them, such as belonging and safety, are not acquirable while some others, such as peace-seeking, are acquirable. However, both types of psychological needs, either acquirable or nonacquirable, depend on specific mental states and the psychological structure of humans.

4. Religion takes shape on the basis of the initial psychological structure of human and it is a contributing factor in the creation of a special psychological structure which compels human to do specific actions.

5. The psychological structure is the central meaning of *shakeleh*; other meanings of *shakeleh* refer to the quality of the psychological structure of human beings. The psychological structure of humans is actually a single set through which the intentions arise, mood is produced, religion is approved, and finally, the needs are expressed and emerged and the self helps *shakeleh* to take shape.

Based on what just mentioned, Ahmadi (2014) is of the belief that *shakeleh* is the human's psychological structure which takes form through the interaction of heredity, environment, and free will, in a way that interprets environmental stimuli in accordance with itself and responds to the stimuli in a specific way. To emphasize and confirm his point of view, Ahmadi (2014) presents the verses

82–84 of the 17th chapter of the Quran and also interpretations of some parts of them:

> And We send down of the Qur'an that which is healing and mercy for the believers, but it does not increase the wrongdoers except in loss. And when We bestow favor upon the disbeliever, he turns away and distances himself; and when evil touches him, he is ever despairing. Say, 'Each works according to his *shakeleh*, but your Lord is most knowing of who is best guided in way'.

These verses show that in proportion to the *shakeleh* they have, the two groups of believers and disbelievers interpreted and responded to a single message and stimulus differently. However, the elated adjective, i.e., "best guided," indicates that the call by *shakeleh* and internal traits to do what they want is not an obligatory invitation that no one can decline; this means that although a person who, for instance, has a *shakeleh* of injustice and wrongdoing is called on by his/her *shakeleh* to display wicked behavior, he/she can slowly and laboriously find the right path.

3.1.2 Qur'anic Theory of Personality

Abu-Raiya (2012) presented a structural theory of personality based on Qur'anic verses and called it the Qur'anic theory of personality. To him, the *nafs* (psyche) means personality, and it encompasses other structures which surround it. These structures are the following: 1. *nafs ammarah besoa'* (evil-commanding psyche), which is evil in nature and it is the strongest force of personality (*nafs*). The evil-commanding psyche resides in the person's unconscious and consists of the forbidden desires and impulses which are managed by the principles of wicked pleasures and initial processing; 2. *al-nafs al-lawammah* (the reproachful psyche), which is ethical in nature and has divine roots and effects; 3. *roh* (spirit), which resides in collective unconscious; 4. *a'ql* (intellect), which has an angelical nature and it is the only conscious component of the system. Intellect is the rational force of the *nafs*, and the ultimate function of it lies in understanding God's essence through its reflections in nature and humankind; 5. *qalb* (heart), which is the heart of the *nafs*. The inputs or messages of other structures of the soul are processed and integrated in the heart, which consequently determines the destiny of the *nafs*; 6. *al-nafs al-mutmainnah* (the serene psyche), which is the ultimate desired outcome of the dynamic interaction between different combinations of *nafs*; and 7. *al-nafs al-marid'a* (the sick psyche), which is a pathological status resulted by a contradictive

AN INTRODUCTION TO ISLAMIC PSYCHOLOGY

deviated and firm heart. These structures and consequences are dynamically related to one another. Being the core of the system, the heart is the gateway to other elements. Intellect receives its input from the outside world, processes this input cognitively, and sends the outcome to the heart.

3.2   Trait Approach to Personality

In the trait approach, the personality of individuals is described through the same method we use for describing people in our daily life. This method makes use of adjectives to describe a person's personality. For instance, one may say "Sina is ambitious" or "Mina is kind." Such categorization of people on the basis of traits has existed since the distant past. Based on internal fluids or "temperaments," Hippocrates introduced four personality types: choleric, melancholic, sanguine, and phlegmatic. Also, in the 1940s, Sheldon proposed another taxonomy of personality, which was based on body type and temperament. However, Cattell, Allport, and Eysenck in the past and the five-factor model of personality and The HEXACO model of personality in the present moment constitute the most important theories in this approach.

Cattell defines personality as the following: something that makes it possible to predict what a person would do in a given situation. He made a distinction between source traits and surface traits. To him, source traits are fewer than surface traits, and they are better predictors of behavior. He considers 16 source traits to be the basic factors of human personality: warm, kind, and adaptable/ cold and reserved; more intelligent/ less intelligent; emotional stability/ affected by feelings; dominant, assertive/submissive, humble; enthusiastic and impulsive/moderate and controlled; conscientious/conforming; bold/shy; sensitive and tender-minded/tough-minded and self-reliant; suspicious/trusting; imaginative/practical; private/forthright; apprehensive and self-doubting/self-assured; experimenting/conservative; self-reliant/group-dependent; tolerant/intolerant; and tense/relaxed. The surface traits are the personality characteristics that correlate with each other but do not form a factor because they are not determined by a single source. For example, several behavioral elements such as anxiety, doubt, and illogical fear combine with each other to form a surface trait, i.e., neuroticism. The neuroticism is not engendered by a single source. Surface traits are not stable and permanent, so they are of little significance in the description of personality (Schutz & Schultz, 2017).

Allport (1961) defined traits as stable and lasting methods of reacting to environmental stimuli. In other words, he believed that personality traits are the tendency towards giving a response to different kinds of stimuli in the same or similar ways. Allport referred to the traits shared by a lot of individuals – such as the people living in the same culture – as the common traits, whereas the traits unique to each person were at first referred to as personal traits but later as personal dispositions. He introduced three types of personal dispositions: cardinal traits, which are pervasive and penetrative and have relations with almost all of the aspects of a person's life, such as blind patriotism; central traits, which include a few numbers of traits that are mentioned when discussing a familiar person, such as aggressiveness and suspicion; and secondary traits, which show up in such a weak and infrequent way that only close friends and family members are aware of that, such as preferring a special type of food or music.

Eysenck (1967), carrying out extensive research for years, suggested a personality theory based on three dimensions, each of which is consisted of a combination of many factors or traits. The personality dimensions in Eysenck's theory include extraversion/introversion, neuroticism/emotional stability, and psychoticism/impulse control (Akbari-Zardkhaneh et al., 2018).

The five-factor model of personality (McCrae & Costa, 1987) is today's representative of the trait approach to personality. In this theory, personality includes five major factors: neuroticism, extraversion, openness, agreeableness, and conscientiousness (Zandi et al., 2017). The instrument mostly used for the assessment of personality in this approach is the NEO-R inventory.

That the adjective words were used to describe personality provoked a lot of discussions. These discussions are because of differences in personal and linguistic interpretations in different cultures. Such differences were not predicted in the five-factor model, so this model ran into the problem of the inability to present a consistent factor structure in different languages. Regarding the Italian, Dutch, Greek, and Filipino languages, research has shown that in the factor analysis studies, either extra factors appeared or a specific dimension of factor analysis was not demonstrated (Church et al., 1997; Di Blas & Forzi, 1998; Saucier et al., 2005; Szirmak & De Raad, 1994, cited in Lobrano, 2014). The investigation into the psychometric properties of this test in Muslim countries revealed that this test has technical issues. Roshan-Chesly et al. (2016) studied the psychometric properties of the mentioned test for a large group of students in universities in Tehran. The results of their tests showed that the factor *openness* lacks a desirable level of internal consistency. The construct validity of the instrument has critical issues too. In a study conducted by Joshanloo, Bakhshi, and Daemi (2013) on 1602 Iranian students, only two factors out of the five major factors were extracted: neuroticism and conscientiousness. Similar findings in other Muslim counties have been reported, including a study by Mastor, Jin, and Cooper (2000) in Malaysia and a study by Halim, Derksen, and

AN INTRODUCTION TO ISLAMIC PSYCHOLOGY   43

Vander Staak (2004) in Indonesia. However, research evidence has shown a consistent five-factor structure for the English language (Ashton & Lee, 2007).

Such issues of the five-factor model of personality provoked researchers into developing a factor structure which not only is founded on the basis of adjective words but also the mentioned limitations are minimized in it; one of these efforts was the Hexaco model developed by Ashton and Lee (2007). In this model, neuroticism is not shown, and the traits and characteristics are divided into two dimensions: *agreeableness* and *emotional stability*. In addition, the characteristics related to the rational ability which existed in the *openness* dimension in the five-factor model were not shown in this dimension of the new model. Perhaps the most significant difference between these two models is that the Hexaco model has an additional dimension: *The Honesty-Humility* dimension, which includes the traits of sincerity, fairness, greed avoidance, and modesty. The emergence of factors like honesty and humility, which are strongly emphasized in Islam, necessitates the development of a trait theory relating uniquely to Muslims for the studies conducted on factor analysis of personality. As one of the rare efforts made within this field, Shojaei et al. (2014) attempted to analyze the content of religious-Islamic texts so as to extract examples of personality traits from Islamic sources.

3.2.1   Trait Theory of Personality from the Islamic Perspective
The following presents one of the personality theories from an Islamic standpoint using the trait approach.

3.2.2   Classification Patterns of Personality Attributes in the Islamic Sources
Shojaei et al. (2014) analyzed the content of religious sciences and extracted different patterns of personality attributes in Islamic sources. According to them, the classification patterns of personality attributes in the Islamic sources is as the following:

Conceptual pattern: the first and simplest classification pattern of personality attributes in the Qur'anic verses and *hadith* is the conceptual pattern. The traits are conceptually divided into three types in this pattern: A) COMMON GENERAL TRAITS: there are some abilities and characteristics which are very general, and the *hadith* and Qur'anic verses have attributed them to human beings. These traits often refer to fundamental and relatively intrinsic characteristics which indicate the distinction between human being and other creatures. Such traits and characteristics can be categorized into two groups: positive traits and negative traits. The positive characteristics can include the following: the capability of serving on Earth as a surrogate for God (Quran 2:30), human's intrinsic honor and dignity (Quran 17:70; 23:14), having the power of making choices (Quran 76:2,3), the existence of a divine and angelical component inside human personality (Quran 89:12; 66:72), God-seeking *fitrah* (Quran 30:30), self-awareness (Quran 75:14,15), perfectionism (Quran 84:6) and tendency towards goodness and kindliness (Quran 91:7,8). The negative characteristics may include the following: committing injustice (Quran 14:34; 18:54), ignorance (Quran 33:72), committing tyranny (Quran 96:6,7; 42:27), weakness and impotence (Quran 4:28), being hasty (Quran 21:37), greed and avarice (Quran 70:19), being stingy (Quran 17:100), and ungratefulness (Quran 41:50); B) COMMON SPECIAL TRAITS: they are the traits that belong to the individuals of a special group, class, or party. For instance, through a categorization based on faith, the individuals were classified into three groups of a believer, disbeliever, and hypocrite, and the moral, cognitive, and social characteristics of each of them were depicted; C) PERSONAL TRAITS: they refer to a set of unique characteristics and also to the distinction between individuals in terms of personal characteristics. For example, some people are used to controlling their anger.

Communication pattern: In this pattern, the personality traits are categorized into four classifications: the traits related to the relationships between the person and his/her self, the traits related to the relationships between the person and other people, the traits related to the relationships between the person and nature, and the traits related to the relationships between the person and God. A) the traits which are related to the relationships between the person and his/her self include self-awareness, self-acceptance, self-worth, patience, and so on; B) the traits which are related to the relationships between the person and other people include friendship, love, intimacy, empathy, good-temperedness, tolerance, modesty, humbleness, etc.; C) the traits which are related to the relationships between the person and environment include the perspective on life, attachment to this world, being dynamic, purposefulness, and so on; and D) the traits which are related to the relationships between the person and God include serving God, sincerity, thanksgiving, patience, reliance on God, having hope toward God, hypocrisy, and the like.

It seems that the main problem of communication pattern is that the traits overlap with one another in a relationship. For example, traits like gratefulness (thankfulness), truthfulness (sincerity), hopefulness (expectance), and despair (hopelessness) are categorized as "relationship between the person and God," whereas these traits can also apply to the relationship between the person and others and the relationship between the person and life in general.

Bipolar pattern: based on some *hadiths*, traits can range from a positive pole to a negative pole, in a way that zero indicates the middle spot. The positive

AN INTRODUCTION TO ISLAMIC PSYCHOLOGY

pole and its opposite side (the negative pole) include Fitrah–Nature, Ruh–Nafs, Reason–Ignorance, Good–Evil, and Piety–Lust.

Tripolar pattern: in addition to the two extremes (one of excess and the other of deficiency) on both sides, a golden mean for each trait has also been taken into consideration in this pattern. According to Imam Ali, the virtues are of four types: *Hikmah* (Wisdom), the basis of which is profound thinking; *Iffah* (Chastity), the basis of which is sensual desires; *Shaja'a* (Bravery), which its basis is anger; and *'Adaala* (Justice), the basis of which is the moderation of sensual forces (cited in Majlesi, 1403 AH, vol. 81:75). However, it is worth noting that this pattern is applicable to the traits which have the modes of excessive, deficient, and moderate, but it cannot be used for traits like justice which has only one side.

Hierarchical pattern: in this pattern, the traits can be classified hierarchically from abstract levels to lower levels. For example, Figure 1 represents the hierarchical pattern of the faith trait on the basis of one of the sayings of Imam Ali. Other traits such as disbelief, hypocrisy, and the like can be drawn through charts similar to this chart.

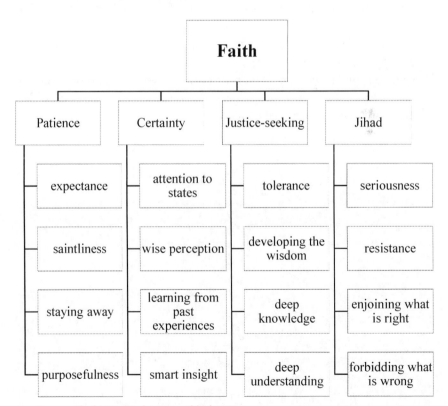

FIGURE 1   The hierarchical pattern of faith trait
ADAPTED FROM KOLINI, 2016, VOL. 3:118; CITED IN SHOJAEI ET AL., 2014: 23

Network pattern: in this pattern, the personality traits are related to one another through a complex network. This pattern is the completed version of conceptual, bipolar, tripolar, and hierarchical patterns and paves the way for using all patterns within a single pattern framework. Each trait in this pattern is viewed as a knot, and the analysis unit is the relations or links which join the knots together. This pattern is identified through two major features: firstly, the meaning of each trait is understood via its relation to other traits. Secondly, this pattern puts emphasis on the dynamic aspect of traits, so that is why a trait or a system of traits (according to the different elements and meanings that they have) may relate to different traits. This pattern has not explicitly received much attention from Islamic sources, but its general grounds exist in these sources, and some researchers have cited examples of it. For example, besides alluding to the bipolar pattern of the virtue of *patience* and its opposite side *impatience* and the tripole of *excess, deficiency*, and *golden mean*, Naraghi (2004, cited in Shojaei et al., 2014) has also discussed a pattern in which a trait on its own is neither virtue nor vice, but that a trait is a virtue or vice depends on the meaning it implies and also on the relation that contextually it has with other words. For instance, fear is sometimes used versus sorrow, sometimes versus hope, and sometimes versus safe, or faith is sometimes used across from disbelief and sometimes across from thankfulness.

Figure 2 shows a very simple representation of network pattern traits. The groups in this figure represent constructs or traits, and the direction of the relationship between them is shown by arrows.

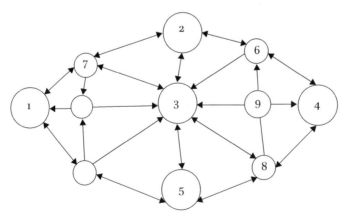

FIGURE 2   A simple example of network pattern of personality attributes
ADAPTED FROM SHOJAEI ET AL., 2014: 25

3.3 *Summary*

Given the nature of man in Islam, it seems that from an Islamic point of view, one can look at personality in two ways. The first view, i.e., structural view on personality, has a long history among Muslim scientists, which was presented in this part, mentioning the theory of personality as "shakeleh" (Ahmadi, 2014) and Qur'anic theory of personality (Abu-Raiya, 2012). The second view, presented in this part via a model designed by Shojaei et al. (2014), is the trait approach to personality.

Shakeleh is the human's psychological structure which takes form through the interaction of heredity, environment, and free will, in a way that interprets environmental stimuli in accordance with itself and responds to the stimuli in a specific way. Verses 82–84 of the 17th chapter of the Quran are the evidence for this definition. These verses show that in proportion to the *shakeleh* they have, the two groups of believers and disbelievers interpreted and responded to a single message and stimulus differently. However, the call by *shakeleh* is not obligatory in a way that no one can decline; this means that although a person who, for instance, has a *shakeleh* of injustice and wrongdoing is called on by his/her *shakeleh* to display wicked behavior, he/she can slowly and laboriously find the right path.

According to Qur'anic theory of personality, *nafs* (psyche) is identical to personality, and it encompasses other structures which surround it. These structures are the following: 1. nafs ammarah besoa' (evil-commanding psyche), which is evil in nature and it is the strongest force of personality (nafs). The evil-commanding psyche resides in the person's unconscious and consists of the forbidden desires and impulses which are managed by the principles of wicked pleasures and initial processing; 2. al-nafs al-lawammah (the reproachful psyche), which is ethical in nature and has divine roots and effects; 3. *roh* (*spirit*), which resides in collective unconscious; 4. *a'ql* (*intellect*), which has an angelical nature and it is the only conscious component of the system. Intellect is the rational force of the *nafs*, and the ultimate function of it lies in understanding God's essence through its reflections in nature and humankind; 5. *qalb* (*heart*), which is the heart of the *nafs*. The inputs or messages of other structures of the soul are processed and integrated into the heart, which consequently determines the destiny of the *nafs*; 6. *al-nafs al-mutmainnah* (*the serene psyche*), which is the ultimate desired outcome of the dynamic interaction between different combinations of *nafs*; and 7. *al-nafs al-marid'a* (*the sick psyche*), which is a pathological status resulted by a contradictive deviated and firm heart. These structures and consequences are dynamically related to one another. Being the core of the system, the heart is the gateway to other elements. Intellect receives its input from the outside world, processes this input cognitively, and sends the outcome to the heart.

Using the trait approach, one can extract various personality attributes through analyzing religious texts. The most important patterns in this regard as introduced by Shojaei et al. (2014) are as follows: *Conceptual pattern* in which the traits are conceptually divided into three types: a) common general traits b) common special traits c) personal traits; *Communication pattern* in which the personality traits are categorized into four classifications: the traits related to the relationships between the person and his/her self, the traits related to the relationships between the person and other people, the traits related to the relationships between the person and nature, and the traits related to the relationships between the person and God; *Bipolar pattern* based on which traits can range from a positive pole to a negative pole; *Tripolar pattern* wherein in addition to the two extremes (one of excess and the other of deficiency) on both sides, a golden mean for each trait has also been taken into consideration; *Hierarchical pattern* based on which the traits can be classified hierarchically from abstract levels to lower levels; *Network pattern* in which the personality traits are related to one another through a complex network.

4 Mental Disorders and Psychotherapy

4.1 *Definition of Mental Health and Mental Illness*

Nelson (2009) believes that generally, there are two major viewpoints on mental health in western psychology: the medical model and the positive model. As the most efficacious view on mental health, the medical model is founded on *Diagnostic and Statistical Manual of Mental Disorders*. In the Diagnostic and Statistical Manual of Mental Disorders, Fifth Edition (DSM-5), a mental disorder is understood as a syndrome whose distinctive feature is the significant clinical distortion of an individual's cognition and behavioral or emotional regulation, which itself reflects the malfunction of biological, psychological, or developmental processes that provide the ground for psychological functioning. Mental disorders are typically accompanied by great upset and functional deficits in social, vocational, or other important activities in a person's life. According to this definition, an expected or culture-based reaction to an ordinary loss or stress such as the death of a beloved person, is not regarded as a mental disorder. Unconventional behaviors and the conflicts between a person and society are not mental disorders unless this deviation or conflict stems from dysfunction in the person. In this edition, mental disorders include neurodevelopmental disorders, schizophrenic and psychotic disorders, bipolar disorder, depression disorder, anxiety disorder, obsessive-compulsive disorder, post-traumatic stress disorder, dissociative disorder, somatic symptoms, and related disorders, eating disorders, elimination disorders, sleep disorders, sexual dysfunction, gender dysphoria, disruptive, impulse-control, and conduct disorders, addictive disorders, neurological disorders, personality disorders, and paraphilic disorders (Diagnostic and Statistical Manual of Mental Disorders, Fifth Edition, 2014). The medical model seems to have some basic beliefs: 1) mental health is the normal status of human function, and it can be defined as a condition in which a person is functioning well with the least personal distress. In other words, a person is healthy when illness is absent; 2. Like physical diseases, mental problems can be classified into more distinctive categories of diseases. Each disease has distinct symptoms which are related to common causes, and the knowledge about the category of disease helps one to employ proper recommendation and treatment; 3. Mental illnesses are abnormal conditions generated from either internal causes or external environmental causes. The internal causes of mental disorders include biological malfunction or the problems existing throughout the developmental period; the external causes may include job loss, perceived threat, and the like; 4. Religious or spiritual themes are not often related to mental health, but they may be the cause or the manifestation of pathology.

The medical model has been criticized by both religious and secular researchers. The most significant examples of these criticisms are the following: 1. That mental health is defined as the absence of illness is a negative approach and ignores the presence or absence of human strengths. In addition, terms like "normal" or "functioning well" are ambiguous; 2. Mental problems are not axiomatic facts, so labeling some things as "abnormal" or "disease" is a judgment dependent on an ideology or a set of cultural values which interpret the meaning of that condition, introduce it as a problem, and recommend solutions for that; 3. Religious or spiritual concerns are very important to mental health, and ignoring religion or having a negative view of it can be a kind of prejudgment and bias.

Dissatisfaction over the medical viewpoint on mental health led psychologists to turn their attention to the positive model of mental health. In this model, mental health is regarded as something more than a lack of illness. Deci and Ryan (2001; cited in Nelson, 2009) believe that the positive models of mental health have two different approaches: in the hedonic approach, mental health equals happiness, i.e., the temporary experience of pleasure and avoiding the negative emotions. This approach is based on the principle that seeking pleasure and avoiding pain are the main motives of humans; the second approach, subjective wellbeing, is related to a person's evaluation of his/her life's quality. In this approach, mental health is seen more as a dynamic process rather than the ultimate status of pleasure. It has sometimes been used under the wide category of psychological wellbeing: a situation in which a person A) engages with life and tries to cultivate skills and find meaning; B) develops the quality of their relationships, and C) improves their competencies and seeks for mastery of the environment. Positive psychology is the most significant school of thought that follows this approach.

It seems that within an Islamic viewpoint, there are two general views on mental health: the first view defines mental health on the basis of the criteria health and disease. According to Aboutorabi (2007), some of the most important criteria of normality and abnormality exist in Islam. The following can be regarded as the criteria of normality: A) dynamic and continuant evolutionary move: in an Islamic viewpoint, normal personality is always undergoing evolution and trying to approach God; B) being purposeful in life: a normal person follows a specific goal throughout all of their behaviors, gives meaning to all of their own ontological dimensions via awareness about divine traditions and laws ruling over the existence, and even considers the afflictions, pains, and sufferings inflicted on them to be for their own good; C) rationality and contemplation: according to religious texts, thinking is one of the most notable signs of believers and normal persons: "Who remember Allah while standing or sitting or [lying] on their sides and give thought to the creation of the heavens and the earth, [saying], 'Our Lord, You did not create this aimlessly; exalted are You [above such a thing]; then protect us from the punishment of the Fire.'" (Quran 3:191); D) calmness of the heart: in the Holy Qur'an, the two terms "comfort" (Surah Ar-Ra'd, verse 28[20]) and "*Sakina*"[21] (Surah Al-Fath, verse 4[22]) are used to describe calmness of the heart.

On the other hand, although lack of thinking is supposed to be the distinct symptom of abnormal persons, "The example of those who disbelieve is like that of one who shouts at what hears nothing but calls and cries cattle or sheep – deaf, dumb and blind, so they do not understand" (Quran 2:171), the criteria of abnormality (based on Islamic texts) can be as the following: A) lack of understanding, thinking, and reasoning; B) deviation and illness of heart; and C) stress. Abnormal individuals are those who do not have an appropriate understanding of the phenomena in their surroundings or those who do

---

20   "Those who believe and whose hearts find comfort in the remembrance of Allah. Surely in the remembrance of Allah do hearts find comfort."

21   *Sakina* means spirit of tranquility, peace and reassurance.

22   "He is the One Who sent down serenity [*Sakina*] upon the hearts of the believers so that they may increase even more in their faith."

AN INTRODUCTION TO ISLAMIC PSYCHOLOGY 51

not properly use the tools of knowledge, i.e., reason and thought, which are bestowed upon them by God, "And We have certainly created for Hell many of the jinn and mankind. They have hearts with which they do not understand, they have eyes with which they do not see, and they have ears with which they do not hear. Those are like livestock; rather, they are more astray. It is they who are the heedless" (Quran 7:179); "... deaf, dumb and blind, so they do not understand" (Quran 2:171); "Indeed, the worst of living creatures in the sight of Allah are the deaf and dumb who do not use reason" (Quran 8:22). In addition, abnormal people are those who "In their hearts is disease, so Allah has increased their disease, and for them is a painful punishment because they [habitually] used to lie" (Quran 2:10); "So you see those in whose hearts is disease hastening into [association with] them, saying, 'We are afraid a misfortune may strike us.' But perhaps Allah will bring conquest or a decision from Him, and they will become, over what they have been concealing within themselves, regretful." (Quran 5:52).

Regarding the *stress* criterion, Islam regards human *fitrah* as something which reaches equanimity and heartily assurance only through having faith in God and afterlife, or it would always be worrying. Verse 124 of chapter 20 and verse 28 of chapter 13 of Quran refer to this: "And whoever turns away from My remembrance – indeed, he will have a depressed life, and We will gather him on the Day of Resurrection blind." (Quran 20:124); "Those who have believed and whose hearts are assured by the remembrance of Allah. Unquestionably, by the remembrance of Allah hearts are assured." (Quran 13:28). According to these two verses, ignorance and turning away from the remembrance of God result in anguish and distress, while remembrance of God results in equanimity. It is worth mentioning that difficulties and strains of life do not refer to economic and financial difficulties, and sometimes a person may have a good financial status while anxiously seeking more and more gratifications.

Within the second view, which corresponds to positive psychology, Hosseini (2008) believes that mental health (in Islam) should be defined on the basis of the foundations of Islam regarding the concepts of "health" and "psyche." In Islam, health is defined via characteristics like prevention priority, true unity, comprehensiveness of plan, balance, making use of human potential, and simplicity. These characteristics exist in the person's balanced and logical relationship with God, self, people, and nature. In addition, out of the terms ruh, nafs, and qalb, the term nafs is closer to "psyche" because when the spirit is separated from the body and its interactions are totally cut off, psychology fades away and also because the heart is mostly related to mental manifestations of human.

Therefore, mental health (in Islam) includes either complete and legitimate satisfaction of needs or treatment and health of *nafs*; it can refer to the legitimate methods and principles which in the first step pave the way for provision, generation, and maintenance of the health of *nafs*, make preparations for *nafs*'s enhancement and evolution in the second step, and prepare the way for the treatment of mental disorders in the third step. The following are the important points of this definition: A) legitimate principles and methods refer to the scientific and pragmatic methods which exist in Islamic commands and, when applied, lead to human's mental health; B) the word "provision" suggests prevention and the words "enhancement" and "evolution" suggest that the mentioned principles not only result in mental equanimity and balance but also they lead human to an evolutionary path. The word "treatment" suggests that the comprehensiveness of Islamic commands, plans, and principles is in a way that these principles can be used in both prevention and treatment steps; C) that the word "*nafs*" is used in the phrase "health of *nafs*" indicates that mental health in Islam does not essentially mean the health of the *ruh* (spirit) or the health of the *qalb* (heart), but "*nafs*" corresponds to the Qur'anic concept of the psyche; D) in this definition, moving towards perfection, reaching perfection, and becoming a perfect human are considered to be the purpose of mental health; E) the words "first step" and "second step" are employed to show that healthy human is different from perfect human (al-Insān al-Kāmil) and if mental health is not provided, reaching perfection would not be possible for a human.

Generally, it seems that the Islamic interpretation of mental health and disorder is rooted in the Islamic perspective on human quiddity. In Islam, human, on the one hand, has a mortal and perishable body, but on the other hand, has an immortal and eternal spirit. The spirit is the most important one, whereas the body is just a frame that is used for breathing God's spirit into it. The functions of *ruh* (spirit) are at three different levels (*qalb*, *nafs*, and *aql*), which should be kept pure and be directed according to Qur'anic commands. It seems that in Islam, the balance between these three functions means mental health, whereas the dominance of one of them over the other leads to mental disorder.

4.2 Religious Psychotherapy in the Islamic Tradition

Psychotherapy refers to "a formal process of interaction between therapist and client for the purpose of amelioration of distress relative to one or more than one of the following areas of disability or malfunction: cognitive functions, affective functions, or behavioral functions by making use of some theories of personality and development, along with methods of treatment logically related to those theories, with professional and legal approval to act as a therapist." (Corsini, 2000).

Jafari (2014) states four major differences between the western psychotherapy system and the Islamic psychotherapy system:

a) Self-fulfilling lifestyle versus righteous benevolence lifestyle: western counseling emphasizes personal progress and satisfaction, competitiveness, interest in oneself, assertiveness, and freedom of choice, so it is a bit self-centered. However, Islam pays attention to a person's rights and freedom but puts more emphasis on principles of mutual responsibility, which is reflected in the concepts of "*ummah*"[23] and "brotherhood". Therefore, Islamic counseling puts emphasis on humility, altruism, and happiness for others instead of self-orientation.

b) Materialistic view versus holistic view: Islam emphasizes holistic progress on both material and spiritual dimensions, i.e., not only is the attention paid to the success achieved on the basis of materialistic goals of life such as financial reward and gaining social status but also self-actualization through adapting personal behaviors and emotions to divine will and satisfaction is emphasized.

c) Total freedom versus limited freedom: in western counseling, individuals are often free to follow personal goals without any religious or ethical limitations; this fact is related to lack of commitment and loyalty and evading responsibility. Within an Islamic framework, freedom is intertwined with the limitations set by *Sharia*[24] on both public and private behaviors. The concepts of *Halal* and *Haram*[25] are clearly elaborated in Islam and this system has worked out well.

Therefore, psychotherapy should be structured in accordance with the worldview of Muslim clients. Several studies have reported the positive outcomes of religious psychotherapy for the treatment of anxiety, depression, and grief in Muslim clients. Within each of these studies, the clients who were in the religious psychotherapy groups responded significantly faster than those who received standard treatment. For example, Masjedi-Arani et al. (2020) examined and provided evidence for the effectiveness of hope therapy with an Islamic approach on reducing the symptoms of anxiety and depression. Their treatment program, formulated in eight sessions, is based on the components

---

23 An Arabic word meaning "community". It is commonly used to mean the collective community of Islamic people. In the Quran the ummah typically refers to a single group that shares common religious beliefs, specifically those that are the objects of a divine plan of salvation.

24 An Islamic religious law that governs not only religious rituals but also aspects of day-to-day life in Islam. It is derived from the religious precepts of Islam, particularly the Quran and the *hadith*.

25 The words "*halal*" and "*haram*" are the usual terms used in the Quran to designate the categories of lawful or allowed and unlawful or forbidden.

of hope in the verses of the Holy Qur'an and the Islamic traditions. The content of these therapeutic sessions includes the following: 1) familiarity with therapists and establishing a therapeutic relationship and familiarity with the cycle of despair; 2) familiarity with the meaning and purpose of life from an Islamic point of view, strengthening the tendency towards it, and understanding the cycle of hope from an Islamic perspective; 3) training for goal-setting skills and determining meaningful, transparent, rational, accessible, and measurable goals; 4) the importance of trust to Almighty God and seeking help from Him; 5) spiritual motivation skills and spiritualizing the goals; 6) strengthening a sense of purposefulness and spiritual progress with an emphasis on processes rather than outcomes; 7) the skills to deal with obstacles, problem solving and flexibility; and 8) conclusion and emphasis on effort for the sake of closeness to Almighty God.

In another study (Sharifi et al., 2013), the positive efficacy of cognitive-behavioral grief therapy with an Islamic approach on the general health of the bereaved people was examined and supported. This treatment program includes attention diversion techniques using dhikr, cognitive reconstruction techniques (such as understanding the reality of the world as being temporary, correct insight into death, the inevitability and irreversibility of death, the concepts of fate and destiny, the pervasiveness of death with emphasis on the verses of the Qur'an and the narrations of the infallibles), finding a meaning in loss and suffering (such as regarding the deceased person as being near the divine mercy and eternal peace), examining and fighting the cognitive errors about calamity and loss based on Islamic teachings (such as the inability to bear loss, catastrophizing and magnifying the calamity, and thinking of calamity as unjust), Islam's behavioral advice in dealing with calamity and bereavement (such as maintaining the relationship with the deceased through almsgiving, prayer and pilgrimage to graves), religious coping strategies in adapting to loss (*reza*,[26] *taslim*,[27] *sabr*,[28] and *tawakkul*[29]), and planning and readjusting to life by recalling the religious themes and narrations about hopefulness, purposefulness of human life, and human responsibilities in the cycle of creation.

26　*Reza* (or *riḍā*) literally means "the fact of being pleased or contented". In religious context, this name is interpreted as satisfaction or "perfect contentment with God's will or decree."

27　*Taslim* means surrendering or submitting one's will to God (Allah).

28　*Sabr* literally means 'endurance' or more accurately 'perseverance' and 'persistence'. In the Islamic context, it refers to the act of remaining spiritually steadfast and to keep doing action when facing opposition or encountering problems and setbacks. It is patience in face of all unexpected and unwanted outcomes.

29　*Tawakkul* is the word for the Islamic concept of the reliance on God or "trusting in God's plan."

AN INTRODUCTION TO ISLAMIC PSYCHOLOGY

In Islamic psychotherapy, cognitive therapy is employed to identify and reform unproductive beliefs or to replace such beliefs with the beliefs that emanate from Islam (Quran and Sunnah). The religious themes and cultural beliefs related to illness may be the subject of discussions, and if a person feels guilty, he/she would be directed toward repentance through the proposed recommendations on methods of reforming personal lifestyle and through a commitment to the Sunnah of Prophet Muhammad (Hamdan, 2008). Hamdan also summarized some useful insights extracted from the Islamic school of thought which can be effective in the process of psychotherapy on religious clients:

1. Understanding the reality of the ephemeral world: being aware of the fact that this world is only a passing stage that takes humans to eternal life in the afterlife can be a useful insight when faced with disaster, pain, and anguish. Such inevitable anguishes are the essence and quiddity of the present life. Predicting and looking at the next life makes it easier to understand the transient nature of this world and to deal with the challenges of this world.

    > And this worldly life is not but diversion and amusement. And indeed, the home of the Hereafter – that is the [eternal] life, if only they knew.
    > Quran 29:64

This special aspect and such an insight can be used for interpreting the non-adaptive thoughts related to disappointment and feelings of being immersed in this world. If the afterworld becomes the person's major concern, the worries and concerns about this world will fade away. When the focus is on the afterworld, the person prepares himself/herself for approaching God in the best way possible, and given that death may come up at any moment, preparation for death should be a process in which the person is always involved. Hence, a Muslim person must always try to achieve success in the afterworld and regard it as his/her ultimate goal.

> Say, 'Shall I inform you of [something] better than that? For those who fear Allah will be gardens in the presence of their Lord beneath which rivers flow, wherein they abide eternally, and purified spouses and approval from Allah. And Allah is Seeing of [His] servants'.
> Quran 3:15

2. Trust in and reliance on God: one of the basic concepts of Islamic beliefs is understanding of the fact that God is able to do anything and manage all affairs. Human cannot go beyond the limitations which God has set

on human beings, because everything runs according to His will and free will. This insight helps human follow God and abide by the commands of God. In fact, such an insight releases the person from anguish and worry because it eliminates the concerns about needs and desires related to this world. Human recognizes that God looks after the person who trusts Him, therefore he/she is assured of God's promise. The result is that the concerns and anxieties vanish or decrease, ease replaces hardship, and fear turns into security, peace, and composure.

> If Allah should aid you, no one can overcome you; but if He should forsake you, who is there that can aid you after Him? And upon Allah let the believers rely.
>
> Quran 3:160

3. Understanding the fact that there is ease after each hardship: in the 5th and 6th verses of chapter 94 of the Quran, God says:

> For indeed, with hardship [will be] ease. Indeed, with hardship [will be] ease.

God states in these verses that there will be ease after each hardship. This fact suggests that the ease which comes up after hardship is greater than the hardship itself. As God has promised, ease comes after each hardship. Sometimes God tests humans with calamity and misfortune, so if a person tolerates and accepts them, the endurance of hardships would be easier for them. Such thoughts are promising for especially the people who feel that their situation would not improve or their problems would not reach a resolution.

4. Concentration on God's blessings: comparing the various blessings from God with what has happened to the person can be useful at the time of anguish. The person should think about the fact that the anguish he/she has faced is very trivial as compared to the blessings God has given to him/her. Such understanding helps the person to be thankful when entangled in poverty, disease, or other kinds of frustration. If this understanding mixes with the perception that hardship and suffering have a goal, it could exert a greater effect on the person. Looking at the people who are in a less desirable status helps individuals recognize that their situation is better than others in terms of general health, physical power and ability, and facilities (e.g. food, clothing, housing, and the like). When individuals bring all blessings (either spiritual or mundane) to attention, the anguishes that they may experience would be alleviated.

AN INTRODUCTION TO ISLAMIC PSYCHOLOGY

5. Remembrance of God and reading the holy Quran: Remembrance of God and reading the holy Quran can have a soothing effect on a human's body, mind, and spirit. This soothing effect can, in fact, reduce stress, worry, and anxiety (Qorbani-Vanajemi, Zandi, Nosrati, & Ghobari-Bonab, 2019). Remembrance of God is also one of the simplest forms of worship and can have different forms, including recalling the names and traits of God, admiring and praising God, and thanking God. The greatest form of remembrance is cited in Quran:

> Those who have believed and whose hearts are assured by the remembrance of Allah. Unquestionably, by the remembrance of Allah hearts are assured.
>
> Quran 13:28

These are in fact the components of Islamic belief which prove to be effective for human and provide the *nafs* with whatever it envies. Another objective of psychotherapy from an Islamic perspective is the return to spirituality for dealing with stressful incidents of life and mental disorders. During psychotherapy, the client may be reminded of establishing daily prayers, reading Quran, frequent remembrance of God, reliance on God, and supplication to God. These methods generally enhance relaxation and the general feeling of well-being.

4.3 *Therapeutic Methods with an Islamic Perspective*

The following are the most important therapeutic methods developed based on Islamic teachings:

4.3.1 Spiritually Multidimensional Psychotherapy

Janbozorgi (2015) argues that the major problem of today's psychotherapies is the lack of attention to the origin of human existence. He believes that although humans' thinking about the origin and ultimate destiny has been taken into account in psychology, and it can be seen in the works of Stanley Hall (1844–1934, Hall's attempt to prove that psychological integrity in adolescence is a revival of the early heavenly ages of human life in which there was coordination between human and nature), Baldwin (1975, that modeling made by children through imitation and playing with significant others represents person's understanding of God), Loder (1998, believing in the fact that God is the ultimate foundation of existence and having interaction with God is necessary for spiritual development) and the like, today's psychotherapy has not explicitly paid attention to the origin of life and life after death which are the basics of human spirituality, so the therapy is often adjusted within the framework of human's relationship with himself/herself and with his/her surrounding existence. Given this critical weak point, Janbozorgi presented a spiritually multidimensional psychotherapy model based on Islamic anthropology.

In this model, "intellectuality" is considered as the main theoretical principle, which includes the three sub-principles of "sublimating self-discipline seeking," "reason assessment," and "reasonableness." The sublimating self-discipline seeking means that when humanity reaches a point where their basic needs are in balance (basic balance), their sublimating needs provoke them to go beyond the present situation and reach a higher level of balance or an optimized balance. This happens when the God-oriented and fitri[30] reason of the person is active. This fitri and God-oriented reason exist in human innately. Therefore, in the process of counseling and therapy, at first, the therapist carries out *reason assessment* to ensure that the person has an acceptable level of rationality, then the therapist uses conscious intellectual stimulation along with different exercises and techniques during the therapy to activate reason, i.e., to help the client reach *reasonableness*.

With the three principles just mentioned, rationality encompasses the human's field of perception. This field includes four subsets which in fact cover the fieldwork of spiritually multidimensional psychotherapy:

a) The principles related to perceived origin. The perceived origin means the person's perception of God. The existence of God as a fact is an ontological matter, but the person's perception of God is a psychological issue which the more it is in line with reality, the more efficacious it would be. The following are some of the principles in this realm which should be taken into consideration during the process of counseling and therapy: A-1) principle of monotheistic feedback: the client is supposed to organize and reform certain thoughts related to the existence of God, the unity of God, and the effect of God on his/her life. In fact, the client should clarify to himself/herself the ways the existence of God can be proved and (if not) the ways it is not denied; A-2) principle of being the direct creation of God: this principle provides the client with a fitri and scheme-based thought about the fact that creation of human actually originates from God, not from parents' relationship and human's intended or unintended pregnancies. By putting forward reasoning of which the client would likely approve, the therapist should try to prove that human is the direct creation of God and that human sets foot on this world by God's will. Acceptance of this fact actually provides the person with a kind of spiritual self-esteem. The client can arrive at the

---

30   Of or related to *fitrah*.

judgment that God has created him/her because He may have had something special to do with him/her; A-3) principle of being under divine nurturing nature of God: this principle ascertains the kind of relationship that exists between human and God. The activation of certain belief about God's divine nurture increases clients' feelings of hope and trust and leads them to feel that God is unconditionally involved in rearing and managing human affairs, including the affairs of themselves too; A-4) principle of being under the guardianship of God: the divine nurturing nature of God is applied irrespective of our wants and beliefs, but acceptance of God's guardianship relies on the will of a human, and God regards Himself as the guardian of those who has faith in Him. The choice over the path of God's guardianship and its consequences should be discussed during a therapy session. The clients might resist accepting God's guardianship because they likely believe that it contradicts their free will and that they may be unable to meet the desires of God; A-5) principle of God's wise and conscious conduct towards human: this principle refers to the fact that God performs all of His actions according to homogeneity between actions and the whole creation, and He never carries out futile and purposeless actions. The word "Allah" has been tens of times used in company with the words *Hakim*[31] and *Alim*,[32] then the outcome of this certain thought would be deep trust in God and it provides the ground for a stable object relation and ego strength to manage behavior.

b) Principles related to perceived existence: the perceived existence means human perception of the world and existence. The human's relationship with others and the world and the effect that this relationship exerts on the formation of human personality has been mentioned in many psychological schools of thought. The following are some of the principles in this realm which should be taken into consideration during the process of counseling and therapy: B-1) principle of seeing the world as a place of passing and trial: paying attention to the client's major thoughts about the world and correcting the cognitive errors in this area can enormously help the person with emotional and behavioral regulation. Setting goals for and constant investment in the world, considering the world as unchangeable, having the feelings of true ownership rather than nominal ownership, the delusion of eternal permanence of the world and ignorance or denial of death, and wrong attributions to the world are considered as some of the detrimental issues in this realm which become

---

31 One of the names of God in Islam, meaning "The All-Wise."
32 One of the names of God in Islam, meaning "omniscient."

the subject of counseling and therapy sessions through psychological techniques. It is worth noting that the psychologist should not encourage either being interested or disinterested in the world because the world is the place in which basic needs of a person are satisfied, and the ground for human perfection in the afterlife is provided, so the psychologist should try to regulate interests and correct inefficacious thoughts, which is a kind of realism; B-2) principle of regulation of the relationship between and interest in the world and others: after intellectual stimulation of certain thoughts about the world, the person is expected to regulate his/her relationship with the existence and the others through activating the spiritual self-care system in a self-disciplining way. The main component of this regulation is the relative emotional stability which does not fade when the person writes down the subjects he/she is interested in; B-3) principle of viewing the world as a place belonging to human: within this principle, worldly life is the farm land for the Hereafter; this means that whatever that is bestowed in this world upon human should be used for human progress and excellence; B-4) principle of seeing the existence as the ground for transcendence: when the method of investment in the subjects related to perceived existence is regulated, attempts should be made to use this ground for building a spiritual world and subliming the human characteristics. The activation of spiritual mechanisms, i.e., purposefulness, valuableness, and giving meaning to actions through practical exercises in them helps the person go beyond materialism, selfishness, and situation; B-5) seeing the world as the ground for harm: self-serving thoughts, selective abstraction with regard to the reality of the world, neglect, and viewing the realities of the world in a maximized and minimized way are the most significant cognitive errors which provide the ground for infliction of harms on human. Awareness of such characteristics of the world can likely decrease vulnerability.

c) Principles related to the perceived self: the next realm in which the person should reconstruct their own psychological system is the relationship between them and their self, i.e., the way they perceive themselves. The following are some of the principles in this area which should be taken into account during the process of counseling and therapy: C-1) principle of taking advantage of divine *fitrah*: according to this principle, human has an inherent guide and a clear plan for an evolutionary move towards transcendence, which is placed inside human by God. This principle necessitates the therapist and the client to direct human purposefulness and motivation towards perfection. The divinity of *fitrah* provides grounds for the ability to trust the internal conscience to correct negative schemes; c-2) principle of considering the rules governing the human's psychological system as stable and fixed: when one is of the belief that the rules which govern the psychological system of human are immutable and fixed, trustworthy models of psychological interventions emerge. For example, the rule that if human possesses purification and piety, i.e., the self-transcendent principle, God would give them the ability to distinguish right from wrong and would ignore their mistakes; c-3) principle of human's possession of free will: directing the client to move away from determinism and get toward free will is an important mechanism. The concepts of *will*, *determination*, and *prediction* which are close to this principle should be taken into account here; c-4) principle of coordination between internal and external locus of control of behavior: according to this principle, the important fact is that the internal locus of control and the external locus of control end to a single source related to the perceived origin and perceived end (afterlife). In Islam, the reason is the internal criterion while the external criterion is the *Sharia* law[33] or a plan devised for human by God who has asked human to act according to that on the basis of free will, understanding, and knowledge; c-5) principle of human vulnerability: the human being is in possession of the two mechanisms of *God-oriented reason* and *unbridled lust*. The psychological system of human beings is prone to be under both internal and external effects. This feature dramatically increases the possibility of human vulnerability.

d) Principles related to perceived end (afterlife): this principle includes the necessity of paying attention to the life after death and its psychological consequences. The following are some of the principles in this realm which should be taken into consideration in the process of counseling and therapy: D-1) principle of making a new sense of death: in this principle, making sense of death is revised, and attempts are made to interpret death as something desirable; D-2) principle of choosing a more genuine, stable, and better life: it is psychologically important that a person acquires the ability to imagine their action's image in the afterlife in a desirable way. Such an exercise directs the person toward meaningful and healthy actions; D-3) principle of meeting God: that afterlife is the personal meeting of all humans with God is considered to be the final attempts to cure human and return human back to action integrity.

---

33   A religious law forming part of the Islamic tradition. It is derived from the religious precepts of Islam, particularly the Quran and the *hadith*. In Arabic, the term *sharia* refers to God's immutable divine law.

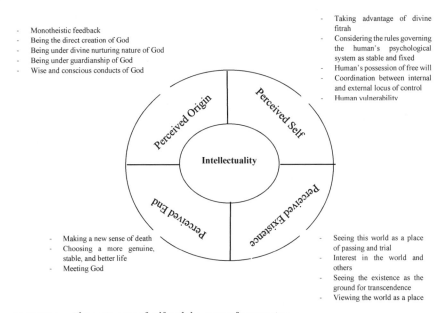

FIGURE 3 The main core of self and the areas of perception
ADAPTED FROM JANBOZORGI, 2015: 37

4.3.2 *Reza* and *Tawakkul*

Pourseyyed-Aghaei (2010) employed this therapeutic method for reducing anxiety and her research provided evidence for its efficacy. This novel remedy included familiarity with the concepts of *reza* and *tawakkul* and the difference between *reza* and the concepts of patience and *tawakkul*, familiarity with types of *reza* and *tawakkul* and the philosophy of them, familiarity with characteristics of those who rely on God (have *tawakkul*) and are satisfied with God's will (have *reza*), acquiring the ability to recognize one's strengths and weaknesses in *reza* and *tawakkul*, acquiring the ability to be satisfied with God's will and relying on God in hardships, recalling the joys (God's blessings) when facing with hardships, familiarity with the effects of *reza* and *tawakkul* on life (divine reward, increase of God's blessings due to having *reza* and *tawakkul* at the times of joy and bliss, calmness and self-esteem, and anger management) and instilling spiritual motive into others.

4.3.3 Islamic Therapy for Grief Intervention

Fattahi, Kalantari, and Molavi (2014) employed this psychotherapy to treat externalizing problems of grief. The therapy sessions generally included cognitive skills (belief in predestination, finding meaning in loss, and divine test), moral skills (*tawakkul*, submission, *reza*, and patience), and behavioral skills

AN INTRODUCTION TO ISLAMIC PSYCHOLOGY 63

(dhikr,[34] invocation, crying, visiting graves, and visiting relatives). Investigating the story of grief, more familiarity with bereavement, understanding the difference in family members' disparate reactions to loss, identifying the bereaved individual's inefficacious feelings and beliefs, the events that provoke unpleasant emotion, making use of writing method for healing, teaching the cycle of thought-emotion-behavior, reviewing the negative thoughts and the challenge of them, referring to *hadiths* and Qur'anic verses at the time of facing with troubles, investigating the relationship with God, discussing about *tawakkul*, instructing the turning of attention by means of *dhikrs* (holy names repetition), supplication and *Tawassul* (requesting the infallible Imams for intercession), discussing about thanatology and the realities of death, correcting wrong beliefs, helping the bereaved to find meaning in calamity, talking about divine decree and test, training mental imagination of phenomena of existence in order to gain positive energy, enhancing the worship-related behaviors, investigating the cognitive distortions, presenting other behavioral techniques like visiting graves, giving to charity, crying, daily plan to invoke God, engaging in social relationships, discussing about the role of patience, *reza*, and submission in dealing with loss, following the infallible Imams as role models when facing hardships, discussing about the necessity of adaptation to new life, investigating religious themes on hope, and the purpose of life are the main topics discussed during sessions.

4.3.4 Monotheistic Integrated Therapy

In this method of therapy, after the observation and clinical diagnosis phase, educational, therapeutic interventions are made through two different, but complementary processes: in the first stage (psychoeducational process), the clients participate in a compact educational course and get familiar with special skills which provide the ground for the therapy sessions. These skills often include self-knowledge, repentance and returning back to the clean *fitrah* of human, interpersonal relationship, problem-solving, establishing religious rituals, saying prayers and having an intimate relationship with God, coping skills, and spiritual and moral skills.

This therapeutic approach emphasizes forming integrity in the client's biological, psychological, social, and spiritual dimensions. With the focus on acceptance of personal responsibility for behavioral abnormalities and

---

34 *Dhikr*, also spelled *Zikr, Thikr, Zekr*, or *Zikar*, literally means "remembrance, reminder" or "mention, utterance". They are Islamic devotional acts, in which holy names, phrases or prayers are repeated. It can be counted on a set of prayer beads or through the fingers of the hand.

besides investigating the intrapersonal characteristics and traits, this model tries to enhance interpersonal relationships, and educate the ways to cope with social tensions and pressures so as to increase satisfaction from a positive relationship with the environment (Mohammadi, Kajbaf, & Abedi, 2014; Sharifinia, 2008).

Jalali Tehrani (2014) has also presented a monotheistic integrated therapy approach which has also received lots of attention. The significant components of this approach are the following:

a) *The therapeutic relationship*: in this method, the therapeutic relationship is very important, and it is regarded as the most important tool for making change. The therapeutic relationship includes two important aspects: A-1) therapist's viewpoint: the views common between Islamic and humanistic approaches regarding the goodness of human nature, the fact that to err is human, tendency and acting toward perfection and development, and being responsible throughout this path have been reflected in the therapist's view. This dimension includes three sub-dimensions: belief, respect, and acceptance; 1-1) *belief*: in this approach, the therapist holds the belief that human being has a clean *fitrah*, has been provoked into perfection, and freely chooses to either move or not move towards this perfection. The ability of and motivation for change is supported by the *nafs*, but they spring from a transcendent source; 1-2) *respect*: the monotheism of the therapist believes that the client is someone who has chosen the therapy to achieve self-actualization, so that's why they are highly respectable; 1-3) *acceptance*: in monotheistic therapy, the therapist is someone who involves in their own process of development, may confront lots of failures and challenges throughout this process, and may achieve some success too. Given that the therapist considers the main reason for possible changes in the client to be something beyond their own role in the therapy, they would not feel arrogant and superior to the client, so the client should accept the therapist as a fellow traveler with whom he/she crosses the path of development and progress. A-2) therapist's approach: the therapist not only should have the aforementioned views, but also they should express those views to the client during the therapy process. The therapist's approach includes three important parts: 2-1) *therapeutic presence*: it refers to the fact that the therapist must make the counselee feel that the presence, attempt, and struggles of the client are the first priority for the therapist and (in order to achieve this goal) the therapist removes whatever that blocks attention to the client (e.g., personal worries, prejudgment about the client, and the like); 2-2) *empathy*: it refers to understanding the client's moods, thoughts, feelings, and contents of reports and the reflection of them

AN INTRODUCTION TO ISLAMIC PSYCHOLOGY 65

by the therapist. In empathy, the therapist must attempt (without making any prejudgments) to understand what the client experiences and present this understanding as a reflection to the client while the client must confirm or correct the therapist's understanding; 2-3) *deep personal eagerness*: it refers to the fact that the therapist's belief that the client is capable of making changes should be transmitted to the client through therapist's words and actions.

b) *Dealing with the contents*: regarding the contents of sessions, the therapy includes the three following factors (These factors occur simultaneously but their ratio change during therapy): B-1) solving the problem: the client's present problem, which has brought pain and sadness on them is regarded as the focus of therapeutic communication. The first task of the therapist is to empathize with the client and look for a solution to reduce the pressure exerted on the client. This solution can include not only the methods of psychological treatment but also referring the client to social workers, referring the client to employment agencies, and the like; B-2) awakening the center of reason and activating the virtues: when the client is on the path to problem-solving, the pressure placed on them will reduce to some extent, and this reduction paves the way to follow their own reason more efficiently when facing different situations. Following the reason helps the client to not only succeed in skill learning and behavior change but also to act in a way that is congruent with their internal nature and generates a feeling of satisfaction. Such actions are self-reinforcing and turn the virtue traits into a kind of personal habit; B-3) integration of meaning: if a person (in different situations of life) confronts virtuous behaviors stemmed from the main center of reason, they will find a different meaning of life. A person who has learned how to solve life problems, trust their own internal reason, and activate their own internal virtues has actually taken a step to create an integrated theme for life.

c) *Maintenance*: permanent and continuant awareness for meaning-making and moving in the direction of monotheism is the major task of the client in this phase. Individuals in this phase are often drawn into a search for transcendent and deeper sources, and they may take on a new commitment to their religion.

4.3.5 Change in Mental Organization Based on Religious Self-Fulfillment Theory

Based on religious self-fulfillment theory, psychological diseases and disorders are the states and features of changed psyches, which have been generated in the process of believing-action and disbelieving-avoidance. For example, imagine a person whom we classify (according to a specific criterion) as 'depressed.' This person has accepted (at a given time) some specific basic beliefs (depressive beliefs) as correct basic beliefs, has put those beliefs into action, and has made such an inclusive change in themselves that we characterize them as 'depressed' at the time they refer to the clinic. By believing in basic depressive beliefs, this person disbelieves the basic ecstatic and cheerful beliefs and avoids them. In the religious self-fulfillment theory, therapy means the modification of the human's essence in all physical and psychological dimensions. In this theory, any mental abnormality always begins with psychological changes; a changed psyche modifies body and brain in accordance with itself. Therefore, the therapy should also begin with psychological activities and remain psychological till the end of the treatment. In the course of therapy, any physical help that seems to be appropriate should also assist the psychological treatment. This is because of the fact that the psyche belongs to the body (especially to the brain), and making any kind of revolutionary changes in the brain will cause changes in psychological moods. Undoubtedly, some of the produced changes help the client deliver a better performance in their psychological activities (put the new basic beliefs into action) and, as a result, move in the desired direction.

The primary premise of the therapeutic technique based on this method is that a special procedure for changing human behavior has been followed in religious sources, and this procedure can be used as a way to provide mental health or as a method of psychotherapy. The steps of implementing this method include the following (Narouei-Nosrati & Mansour, 2009): *First*: formation of some faith units or basic beliefs: there are lots of basic beliefs inside every person and the psyche moves within the corridor of active basic beliefs at a given moment, not within all the basic beliefs that a person inherently has accepted as certain beliefs from the beginning of their life. With a little change in the content or mechanism of a basic belief, the psyche begins to change. Therefore, the first step of psychotherapy is to identify the active basic beliefs within which the person's psyche moves now and to distinguish the correct and right basic beliefs from wrong and incorrect ones; *Second*: acting in accordance with each basic belief or faith unit: after those correct basic beliefs are identified, it is necessary to have faith in them, view them as the strategic plan of actions, and act accordingly. *Third*: denying those basic beliefs which contradict healthy basic beliefs: negating and disbelieving the incorrect and disease-causing beliefs is one of the basic concepts of religious self-fulfillment theory. During the long time that humans believed the Earth was the center of the solar system, they were, in fact, implicitly denying anything other than that. For this reason, when Galileo Galilei claimed that the Sun is the center of the solar system and the Earth orbits that, he was taken to court and had

AN INTRODUCTION TO ISLAMIC PSYCHOLOGY

to recite his abjuration out of fear. Resisting against Galilei's thought was not just because they did not know that the Earth revolves around the Sun, but because they had faith in Sun's orbit around the Earth and nothing else; *Fourth*: avoiding the incorrect matters: abstaining from and not acting according to the incorrect basic beliefs that someone has followed and performed for years is the fourth pillar of this intervention. According to religious self-fulfillment theory, coming to faith in basic beliefs, denying the incorrect basic beliefs, and avoiding the incorrect matters are intertwined, and humans are fulfilling themselves through this mechanism at every moment.

4.3.6   Islamic Multifaceted Treatment

Identifying and knowing oneself with an emphasis on the fact that self-knowing is one of the most profitable examples of knowledge, providing the ground for psychological readiness of a person to investigate thoughts, beliefs, and affections (rejecting the sensual desires, establishing relationships with one's thoughts, and harboring doubts about feelings of dissatisfaction with life and negative attitudes towards others), distinguishing the right thoughts and affections from incorrect ones and accepting them (recognizing the wrong thoughts and understanding the incorrect and erroneous affections), changing one's incorrect thoughts and affections and replacing them with correct ones (strengthening the will, nurturing the patience, developing the certain knowledge, reciting the *dhikr* of "There is no power no strength except from God" and internalizing its concept into oneself), and preventing and inhibiting the relapse of incorrect thoughts and feelings are the most significant instructions of this therapeutic method. Mehrabizadeh-Honarmand, Hashemi, and Basaknejad (2011) used this method to treat depression.

4.3.7   Cognitive-Behavioral Psychotherapy Program Based on Religious Teachings

Khodayarifard et al. (2009) used this therapeutic program to decrease psychological maladjustments in a group of prisoners. This training program was scheduled to have 16 therapy sessions and its techniques were based on religious teachings, including unconditional love on the basis of Qur'anic verses and *hadiths*, coping with disappointment and helplessness, detrimental attributional styles, and getting over cognitive distortions based on Qur'anic verses and *hadiths*, religious coping methods, methods of respecting and trusting oneself, and learning about sources of self-knowledge.

Faghihi and Khodayarifard (2003) recommended cognitive-behavioral therapy based on Islamic teachings to treat depression. The process of this recommended treatment included two general stages: self-knowledge and self-change.

a) *Self-knowledge*: in this stage, the depressed person receives help to become aware of their own attitudes, beliefs, and thoughts. This awareness is useful for distinguishing between right thoughts and attitudes and the wrong ones. This stage includes the following steps: A-1) psychological readiness to investigate the beliefs: mental readiness can be reached via different techniques. For example, the person might be asked to pay attention to each of their own thoughts and deeply think about them, because thinking makes thoughts clear; the person might be asked to question themselves about the reason behind each of their thoughts, and the therapist helps the depressed person to find out that their thoughts are illogical; the person might be asked to be like a bystander and just watch themselves and their own thoughts, look at them from the outside and think about the fact that how s/he would assess those thoughts if they belonged to another person; the person might receive help to investigate more deeply into the causes of an event or a failure rather than probing into what they have attributed to themselves or others which have generated a negative attitude in them. For example, instead of putting the blame on others, the person questions their own performance. A-2) distinguishing right from wrong: in this stage, the client is helped to discriminate incorrect thoughts from correct and logical thoughts and to consider the possibility that they may have incorrect thoughts. A-3) accepting one's erroneous thoughts: establishing the ground for acceptance of erroneous thoughts by the depressed person includes the following steps: conversation, asking and answering questions along with logical guidance helps the client find out that their thoughts are incorrect. In this stage, the client should express the outcomes and consequences of each of their thoughts, and then (with the help of the therapist) they compare logical thoughts with illogical ones so as to pave the way for abandoning the illogical thoughts; attempts should be made to make the client aware of the fact that they have chosen many of these thoughts unthinkingly and without a deep contemplation; the client should also pay attention to the fact that many of the thoughts they consider to be correct are in fact incorrect, so a new look and scrutiny are needed. A-4) keeping away from immature thoughts: after the client discerns their own immature thoughts and finds out that their thoughts are incorrect, they, with the help of the therapist, should avoid dealing again with these thoughts. A-5) accepting the relationship between negative attitudes and depression: in this stage, the client should be helped to discover the relationship between illogical thoughts and their depression.

b) *Self-change*: the client in this stage is assisted to do the following activities: B-1) replacing the incorrect and wrong thoughts with correct ones: in this

AN INTRODUCTION TO ISLAMIC PSYCHOLOGY

stage, the individual should be helped to find right and rational thoughts and substitute wrong and irrational thoughts with them. B-2) noticing the relationship between mature thoughts and mental tranquility: attempts should be made to make the client realize that mature thought helps them remove their doubts, reach a much better thought and opinion, and arrive at emotional and affective calmness. B-3) preventing the relapse of immature thoughts: this prevention is possible through the following ways: frequent repetition of deep logical thoughts; mental engagement and wholehearted attention to God; nurturing the person's self-esteem and creating the belief that illogical thoughts are worthless. To nurture the person's self-esteem, the following methods can be used: a) positive-thinking or identifying the strong points of individuals; b) turning the client's attention to the fact that the greatest of all creatures is the human being because God has breathed His spirit into human's body; c) emphasizing the fact that human's honor is seen by God as desirable while human's disgrace is undesirable for God; d) introducing some exemplary persons for self-esteem and showing their valuable thoughts and behaviors; providing the facilities required to succeed.

4.3.8   Positive Thinking with Emphasis on the Islamic Perspective

Khodayarifard et al. (2016a) suggested a theoretical framework on positive thinking from an Islamic view which could be of use in psychotherapy. They believe that positive thinking implies having positive interpretations about past events, automatic positive thought about present events, and positive expectancies about future events in four areas: relationship with self, relationship with others, relationship with God/holy entity, relationship with nature. Positive thinking manifests in the psychological, biological, social, and spiritual model, and the manifestations of this construct are represented in cognitive, emotional, and behavioral dimensions. Based on the definition just mentioned, the events and happenings are divided into four parts: first, the ones that are in the realm of individual's perceptions of their own abilities; this can be interpreted as the relationship with self. For example, such events among students may include continuing their education and finding friends, jobs, and spouse. The second part is related to the matters in which others have a share; here, *others* mean friends, family, and any individuals who have a close relationship with the person. The third part of these relationships is related to the events that are associated with nature and the surrounding environment, such as nature conservation and natural events like earthquakes, floods, and the future of Earth and the universe. The last and final part is related to human's relationship with holy and extraterrestrial matters; these matters are labeled as the *relationship with God* and include

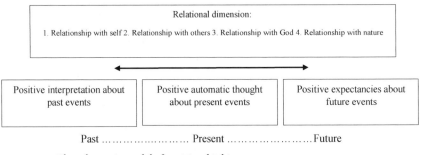

FIGURE 4 The schematic model of positive thinking
ADAPTED FROM KHODAYARIFARD ET AL., 2016A

issues like supplication, hereafter, accepting repentance, and death, which are otherworldly matters. Based on what was just mentioned, the schematic model of positive thinking can be presented on the basis of its temporal and relational dimensions.

a) *Relationship with God*: in times of hardship, optimistic individuals resort to God and other coping methods such as supplication and *tawakkul*, have a positive evaluation of the events in relation to God, and accept the wishes of God. Since such individuals are hopeful about the future, they use patience, as a coping method, in difficult situations and believe that patience and success are two old friends who give meaning to life mishaps. In addition to having a positive outlook on the future, such persons reflect positive aspects at the time of making interpretations. They draw pleasant incidents toward themselves through positive expectations. A positive attitude toward occurrences affects the unconscious mind and cultivates positive dreams, images, and imaginations in a person's mind.

Some examples of this kind of positive expectation likely exist in the stories of the prophets in the Quran. The prophets have positive expectations of God, and these positive expectations help them carry out their prophecy without being afraid of oppositional groups, rely on the help and support provided by God, and regard God as a safe haven and secure base. In this regard, the story of Prophet Abraham can be mentioned as an example; Quran portrays Abraham coming out of the fire. This narrative clearly reveals the prophets' positive thinking. Abraham has such a positive picture of God and God's favors that he seemingly sees fire as a garden; this positive picture and belief also manifest itself in the real world, and the fire turns into cold and safety.[35] Such a positive belief in God, who is the Creator of all the universe, equips the person with such strength and safety that they find themselves in God's arms at every moment and come to the belief that God would save humans from calamities.

---

35   We ordered, "O fire! Be cool and safe for Abraham!" (Quran 21:69).

A lot of religious beliefs, such as expecting a savior, which exists almost in all religions, have emerged out of positive thinking, and this indicates the reality that divine religions have always persuaded their followers into positive thinking. The positive thinking about human's relationship with God is also reflected in the names of God in Islam. The believers see God as a forgiver of sins, benign, compassionate, and merciful. It is worth mentioning that the positive attitude toward God or holy entities can generate hope and strength to fight against physical problems like pain tolerance and difficult-to-treat diseases like cancer, and it can even ease confrontation with psychological problems like depression and anxiety. Another extraterrestrial matter is death; the attitude of a positive thinker toward death is thoroughly different from that of a pessimistic person. A positive thinking person considers death to be the moment of meeting the beloved; he/she is not afraid of death, but pursues it enthusiastically (Zandi, Rahimi, & Mousavi-Nasl, 2021). Some verses of a Qur'anic chapter (89:26–30) allude to this enthusiasm:

> Allah will say to the righteous, 'O tranquil soul!' * Return to your Lord, well pleased with Him and well pleasing to Him. * So join My servants, * and enter My Paradise.

The fact that every person's attitude toward death stems from their own actions, behavior, and positive/negative thinking can be vividly observed in the poems of Rumi, the distinguished Iranian poet (Masnavi-ye-Ma'navi, 3rd book, verses 3439–3442):

> Every one's death is of the same quality as himself, my lad
> to the enemy (of God) an enemy, and to the friend (of God) a friend.
>
> Your fear of death in fleeing (from it) is (really)
> your fear of yourself. Take heed, O (dear) soul!
>
> 'Tis your (own) ugly face, not the visage of Death
> your spirit is like the tree, and death (is like) the leaf.
>
> If you are wounded by a thorn, you yourself have sown
> and if you are (clad) in satin and silk, you yourself have spun.

Generally, in the eyes of the individuals who are securely attached to God, existence is a beautiful manifestation of God's reflection which brings joy and blessing. This optimistic view is plainly portrayed in Qur'anic tales of prophets; the prophets viewed God as a safe haven and secure base and believed that God is always available and supports them at any given time.

b) *Relationship with self:* positive thinkers have a positive attitude toward their own abilities and focus on positive events rather than the failures and concerns related to undesirable events in the past. Such individuals attribute their success and prosperity to their own abilities, rely on their internal resources when facing difficult life situations, and activate their positive and constructive coping strategies to fight against problems (Ahmadi et al., 2018; Ahmadi et al., 2021). Positive thinking individuals have an internal locus of control (Khodayarifard et al., 2017). They believe in close relationships with God and spiritual resources and have a high degree of self-esteem and self-worth. Not only are they hopeful about their own abilities to do something in the future, but also they adopt a positive interpretation of even their failures in the past and seemingly believe in the famous adage, "failure is the pillar of success."

c) *Relationship with others:* When having relationships with other people, positive thinkers mainly pay more attention to the positive aspects of behaviors, observe signs of other individuals' personality development and preparedness for higher levels of life in every attempt that others make, and consider destructive behaviors to be some peripheral events with no fundamental basis. Positive thinkers believe in a philosophy based on human altruism and hold the opinion that human being (if psychologically secured and mentally free of fear and inferiority) is inherently altruistic and likes to connect positively to others and establish a mutual affective relationship with other people. They think positively about observing the rights of other people, such as benevolence, kindliness, and forgiveness, and consider such behaviors to be helpful in actualizing their own internal talents for removing relationship obstacles and nurturing human relationships. In other words, they know that forgiving other people helps them pull free of sufferings, suspicions, and upsets. Instead of regarding the bad behaviors of other people as essential properties of them, positive thinkers believe that such behaviors are accidental properties of people which are produced due to lack of or damages to their controlling spiritual system.

d) *Relationship with nature:* positive thinking individuals believe that the whole existence proceeds through an evolutionary process. The unpleasant events have a specific meaning and concept. The positive thinkers' expectations of natural events and disasters are positive and toward the perfection of spirituality. They have an admiring look at nature and consider natural events to be in line with the purpose of Creation. The people who view nature as the sign of God, immerse in the beauties of nature, and have a feeling of spiritual astonishment are the ones who are connected to existence and believe that existence and nature are reminders of God.

4.4 *Summary*

– It seems that the western psychotherapy approaches focus heavily on symptoms of psychological disorders, and their therapeutic goal is to reduce these symptoms. Therefore, their therapeutic interventions apparently may have a short-term effect, whereas the ultimate goal of therapy in an Islamic perspective is not to simply change the thought, emotion, or behavior, but to have an effect on the *nafs*, in a way that this effect is able to affect other variables such as thought, emotion, or behavior. It is worth noting that along with the main path of western psychology, integration of spiritual and religious themes within therapeutic processes has also been emphasized within the framework of "theistic psychotherapy." The philosophical foundations of this approach include scientific theology, theistic holisticism, human agency, theistic relationism, and altruism. However, the features which distinguish western psychotherapy from Islamic psychotherapy include a self-fulfilling lifestyle versus righteous benevolence lifestyle, materialism versus holisticism, total freedom versus limited freedom, and justification of sins versus repentance and attention to origin and end.

– Spiritually Multidimensional Psychotherapy is one of the most important therapeutic models based on the Islamic framework. In this model, "intellectuality" is considered as the main theoretical principle. Intellectuality encompasses human perception. It includes four subsets: A) The principles related to perceived origin, including the principle of monotheistic feedback, principle of being the direct creation of God, principle of being under divine nurturing nature of God, principle of being under guardianship of God, and principle of God's wise and conscious conduct towards human; B) The principles related to perceived existence, including the principle of seeing the world as a place of passing and trial, principle of regulation of relationship between and interest in the world and others, principle of viewing the world as a place belonging to human, principle of seeing the existence as the ground for transcendence, and principle of seeing the world as the ground for harm; C) The principles related to perceived self, including the principle of taking advantage of divine *fitrah*, principle of considering the rules governing the human's psychological system as stable and fixed, principle of human's possession of free will, principle of coordination between internal and external locus of control of behavior, principle of human vulnerability; D) Principles related to perceived end or afterlife, including the principle of making a new sense of death, principle of choosing a more genuine, stable, and better life, and principle of meeting God.

– Monotheistic Integrated Therapy is another therapeutic model based on Islamic teachings. The most significant components of this approach are the following: A) *Therapeutic relationship* is the most important tool for making change and includes therapist's viewpoint (belief, respect, and acceptance) and therapist's approach (therapeutic presence, empathy, deep personal eagerness); B) *Dealing with the contents*, including solving the problem, awakening the reason, activating the virtues, and meaning unification; C) *Maintenance* refers to permanent and continuant awareness for moving in the direction of monotheism.

– Cognitive-Behavioral Therapy based on Islamic Teachings is another therapeutic model. The process of this model includes two general stages: self-knowledge and self-change; A) *self-knowledge*: This stage includes the following steps: psychological readiness to investigate the beliefs, distinguishing right from wrong, accepting one's erroneous thoughts, keeping away from immature thoughts, and accepting the relationship between negative attitudes and depression; B) *self-change*: this stage includes the following steps: replacing the incorrect and wrong thoughts with correct ones, noticing the relationship between mature thoughts and mental tranquility, and preventing the relapse of immature thoughts through wholehearted attention to God and His attributes.

Acknowledgments

We extend our sincere gratitude to Professor Ralph W. Hood, editor for the series, Brill Research Perspectives in Religion and Psychology, for his invaluable help and encouragement, and his support of this work. We would also like to thank Mrs. Nastaran Rezaei for her great help to us in searching for resources and proofreading. Moreover, we would like to thank Brill for disseminating this work and all other culturally based contributions to psychology. We also appreciate Brill's reviewers whose insightful critique enabled us to improve the quality of this monograph.

References

Aboutorabi, A. (2007). *Criticism of the criteria of normalcy in psychology from the perspective of Islamic resources*. Qom: Publication of Imam Khomeini Education and Research Institute. [In Persian]

Abu-Raiya, H. (2012). Towards a systematic Qura' nic theory of personality. *Mental Health, Religion & Culture*, 15(3), 217–233. https://doi.org/10.1080/13674676.2011.640622.

Ahmadi, A. (1989). *Personality psychology from Islamic perspective*. Tehran: Amirkabir. [In Persian]

Ahmadi, F., Khodayarifard, M., Zandi, S., Khorrami-Markani, A., Ghobari-Bonab, B., Sabzevari, M., & Ahmadi, N. (2018). Religion, culture and illness: a sociological study on religious coping in Iran. *Mental Health, Religion & Culture, 21*(7), 721–736. doi: 10.1080/13674676.2018.1555699.

Ahmadi, F., Cetrez, Ö. A., Akhavan, S., & Zandi, S. (2021). Meaning-Making Coping with COVID-19 in Academic Settings: The Case of Sweden. *Illness, Crisis & Loss.* https://doi.org/10.1177/10541373211022002.

Akbari-Zardkhaneh, S., Poursharifi, H., Yaghubi, H., & Zandi, S. (2018). Five-Dimensional Personality Test: Development and Validation of a Persian Version. *Psychological Studies, 63*(3), 219–227. doi: 10.1007/s12646-018-0457-7.

Alitaba-Firouzjay, R. (2016). Methodology of Islamic Humanities (coordinates, requirements, and characteristics). *Zehn, 17*(68), 147–176. [In Persian]

Ashton, M. C., & Lee, K. (2007). Empirical, theoretical, and practical advantages of the HEXACO model of personality structure. *Personality and Social Psychology Review, 11*(2), 150–166. https://doi.org/10.1177/1088868306294907.

Azarbayjani, M. (2011). *Psychology of religion from William James' perspective.* Qom: Research Institute of Hawzah and University. [In Persian]

Azarbayjani, M. (2020). *Philosophy of Psychology.* Qom: Research Institute of Hawzah and University. [In Persian]

Azarbayjani, M., & Shojaei, M. (2019). *Psychology in Nahj al-Balagha.* Qom: Research Institute of Hawzah and University. [In Persian]

Badri, M. (1979). *The dilemma of Muslim psychologists.* Muslim Welfare House London.

Badri, M. (2016). *Cultural and Islamic adaptation of psychology: A book of collected papers.* Human Behaviour Academy.

Bagheri, K. (2004). Metaphysical Foundation of Islamic Thought for Developing Human Sciences (Emphasizing Psychology). *Clinical Psychology & Personality, 1*(7), 56–70. [In Persian]

Bagheri, K., & Khosravi, Z. (2006). A comparative study of human agency in the Islamic theory of action and critical theory, Habermas. *Wisdom and Philosophy, 2*(7), 7–22. doi: 10.22054/wph.2006.6674.

Bandura, A. (2008). Reconstrual of free will from the agentic perspective of social cognitive theory. In J. Baer, J. C. Kufman, & R. F. Bumeister (Eds.), *Are we free? Psychology and free will* (pp. 86–127). Oxford: Oxford University Press.

Blaikie, N., & Priest, J. (2017). *Social Research: Paradigms in Action.* Wiley.

Bostan, H. et al. (2009). *A step towards religious science: the empirical structure and possibility of religious science.* Qom: Research Institute of Hawzah and University. [In Persian]

Breen, L., & Darlaston-Jones, D. (2008). Moving beyond the enduring dominance of positivism in psychological research: an Australian perspective. Paper presented at the 43rd Australian Psychological Society Annual Conference.

Cohen, L., & Manion, L. (1994). *Research methods in education* (4th ed.). Routledge.

Copleston, F. (2014). *A History of Philosophy, Vol. 5: Modern Philosophy – The British Philosophers from Hobbes to Hume*. Translated by A. Alam. Tehran: Elmi Farhangi Publishing. [In Persian]

Corsini, R. J. (2000). Introduction. In R. J. Corsini & D. Wedding (Eds.), *Current Psychotherapies*. Itasca, IL: F. E. Peacock Publishers, Inc.

Creswell, J. W. (2003). *Research design: Qualitative, quantitative, and mixed methods approaches* (2nd ed.). SAGE Publications.

Creswell, J. W., & David Creswell, J. (2018). *Research Design: Qualitative, Quantitative, and Mixed Methods Approaches* (5th ed.). SAGE Publications.

Ejei, J. (2012). *Psychology from the perspective of Islamic scientists*. Tehran: Daftar-e Nashr-e Farhang-e Islami. [In Persian]

Faghihi, A., & Khodayarifard, M. (2003). The effectiveness of cognitive-behavioral therapy of depression with an emphasis on Islamic view. *Pazhouheshname-ye Quran va Hadith, 1*(2), 89–112. [In Persian]

Fattahi, R., Kalantari, M., & Molavi, H. (2015). The Comparison between the Effectiveness of Islamic Grief Therapy and Group Grief Therapy Program on the Behavioral and Emotional Problems of Adolescent Mournful Girls. *Studies in Islam and Psychology, 8*(15), 39–64. [In Persian]

Flick, U., von Kardorff, E., & Steinke, I. (2004). *A companion to qualitative research*. London: Sage Publications.

Forqani, M., Nouri, N., & Sheikh-Shoaei, A. (2014). A look at Islamic psychology. Qom: Research Institute of Hawzah and University. [In Persian]

Ghobari-Bonab, B., Nosrati, F., Qorbani-Vanajemi, M., & Zandi, S. (2019). A psychological reading of Isra and Miraj. *Rooyesh-e-Ravanshenasi, 8*(3), 157–166. http://frooyesh.ir/article-1-1734-en.html. [In Persian]

Halim, M. S., Derksen, J. J. L., & van der Staak, C. P. F. (2004). Development of the revised-neo personality inventory for Indonesia: A preliminary study. In B. N. Setiadi, A. Supratiknya, W. J. Lonner, & Y. H. Poortinga (Eds.), *Ongoing themes in psychology and culture: Proceedings from the 16th International Congress of the International Association for Cross-Cultural Psychology*. https://scholarworks.gvsu.edu/iaccp_papers/242.

Hamdan, A. (2008a). The prevalence and correlates of depressive symptoms among Arab women in a primary health care setting. *International Journal of Psychiatry in Medicine, 38*(4), 453–467. DOI: 10.2190/PM.38.4.e.

Hamdan, A. (2008b). Cognitive restructuring: An Islamic perspective. *Journal of Muslim Mental Health, 3*(1), 99–116. https://doi.org/10.1080/15564900802035268.

Hamdan, A. (2011). *Psychology from the Islamic perspective*. International Islamic Publishing House IIPH.

Hasani, M. (2012). An Introduction to Mixed Methods in Interdisciplinary Social Sciences. *Interdisciplinary Studies in the Humanities, 2*(4), 137–153. doi: 10.7508/isih.2010.08.007. [In Persian]

Hofstede, G., & Hofstede, G. J. (2005). *Culture and Organization: Software of the Mind* (2nd). New York: McGraw Hill.

Hogan, R., Johnson, J. A., & Briggs, S. R. (Eds.), (2005). *Handbook of Personality Psychology*. San Diego, CA: Academic Press.

Hood, R. W. Jr. (in press). William James and the (non) replication crisis in psychology: conjectures and controversy in the psychology of religion. *Research in the Social Scientific Study of Religion, 33*.

Hoseini, S. (1999). *Collection of analytical theoretical articles*. Shiraz: Shiraz University Publications. [In Persian]

Iman, M. (2011). *Paradigmatic foundations of quantitative and qualitative research methods in the humanities*. Qom: Research Institute of Hawzah and University. [In Persian]

Iqbal, N., & Skinner, R. (2021). Islamic psychology: Emergence and current challenges. *Archive for the Psychology of Religion, 43*(1), 65–77. https://doi.org/10.1177/00846 72420983496.

Jafari, M. F. (1993). Counseling values and objectives: A comparison of Western and Islamic perspectives. *The American Journal of Islamic Social Sciences, 10*(3), 326–339.

Jalali-Tehrani, S. (2004). The monotheistic integrated therapy (MIT). *Naqd Va Nazar, 9*(35–36), 17–46. [In Persian]

Janbozorgi, M. (2015). Principles of Spiritually Multidimensional Psychotherapy (SMP). *Islamic Psychology, 1*(1), 9–45. [In Persian]

Javadi-Amoli, A. (2010). Human natural instinct in Quran. *Religious Anthropology, 7*(23), 5–28. [In Persian]

Joshanloo, M., Bakhshi, A., & Daemi, F. (2014). Survey of NEO-FFI Application for Measurement of Five Main Personality Factors in Iran. *Clinical Psychology & Personality, 2*(9), 95–106. [In Persian]

Kafi, M. (2014). The Islamic Methodological Paradigm of Human Sciences. *Journal of Islam and Social Sciences, 6*(11), 25–51. [In Persian]

Kaplick, P. M., & Skinner, R. (2017). The evolving Islam and psychology movement. *European Psychologist, 223*(3), 198–204. https://doi.org/10.1027/1016-9040/a000297.

Kasule, O. H. (2010). Knowledge: An Islamic perspective. *Journal of the Indian Medical Association, 42*, 50–53.

Kaviani, M. (2019). *Psychology in the Qur'an: Concepts and Teachings*. Qom: Research Institute of Hawzah and University. [In Persian]

Khodayarifard M., Yonesi J., Akbari Zardkhaneh S., Fagihi A. N., Behpajouh A. (2010). Group and Individual Cognitive Behavioral Therapy Based on Prisoners' Religious Knowledge. *Journal of Research in Psychological Health, 3*(4), 55–68. [In Persian]

Khodayarifard, M., Ghobari-Bonab, B., Akbari-Zardkhaneh, S., Zandi, S., Zamanpour, E., & Derakhshan, M. (2016a). Positive psychology from Islamic perspective. *International Journal of Behavioral Sciences, 10*(1), 29–34. http://www.behavsci.ir/article_67938.html.

Khodayarifard, M., Akbari-Zardkhaneh, S., Ghobari-Bonab, B., Shokouhi-Yekta, M., Afrooz, G., Faqihi, A., Tahmasb-Kazemi, B., & Zandi, S. (2016b). Effectiveness of religious-based life skills training on religiosity of university students: A pilot study. *Islamic Psychology*, 2(2), 9–31. http://psychology.riqh.ac.ir/article_12436.html. [In Persian]

Khodayarifard, M., Ghobari-Bonab, B., Shokouhi-Yekta, M., Tahmasb-Kazemi, B., Faghihi, A., Azarbayejani, M., ... Alavinezhad, S. (2019). Religiosity interactional program for university students: Development and validation. *Positive Psychology*, 4(4), 69–84. doi: 10.22108/ppls.2019.112822.1519. [In Persian]

Khodayarifard, M., Zandi, S., Hajhosseini, M., & Ghobari-Bonab, B. (2017). Efficacy of Positive Thinking Training on the Family Process and Subjective Wellbeing of Female Heads of Household. *Journal of Family Research*, 12(4), 593–612. http://jfr.sbu.ac.ir/article_97448.html?lang=en. [In Persian]

Khosravi, Z., & Bagheri, K. (2005). Towards Islamic Psychology: An Introduction to Crossing Theoretical Barriers. *Psychological Studies*, 1(4), 161–172. [In Persian]

Khosropanah, A. (2012). What is the philosophy of the humanities? *Journal of Mirror of Wisdom*, 31, 8–32. [In Persian]

Kuhn, T. S. (1962). *The structure of scientific revolutions* (3rd ed.). University of Chicago Press.

Lobrano, M. T. (2014). *Psychopathy and the HEXACO personality Model.* Doctoral dissertation, Louisiana Tech University. https://digitalcommons.latech.edu/dissertations/260.

Lotfi, H. (2002). Is Islamic Psychology Possible? *Methodology of Social Sciences and Humanities*, 7(29), 5–35. [In Persian]

Manteghi, M. (2018). An investigation in methodology of scientific Ijtehad and its application in Islamic management. *Journal of Public Administration Perspective*, 9(35), 139–157. [In Persian]

Masjedi-Arani, A., Yoosedee, S., Hejazi, S., Jahangirzadeh, M., Jamshidi, M. A., Heidari, M., & Farhoush, M. (2020). Effectiveness of an Islamic approach to hope therapy on hope, depression and anxiety in comparison with conventional hope therapy in patients with coronary heart disease. *Journal of Advances in Medical and Biomedical Research*, 28(127), 82–89.

Mastor, K. A., Jin, P., & Cooper, M. (2000). Malay Culture and Personality: A Big Five Perspective. *American Behavioral Scientist*, 44(1), 95–111. https://doi.org/10.1177/00027640021956116.

McCrae, R. R., & Costa, P. T. (1987). Validation of the five-factor model of personality across instruments and observers. *Journal of Personality and Social Psychology*, 52(1), 81–90. https://doi.org/10.1037/0022-3514.52.1.81.

Mehrabizadeh-Honarmand, M., Hashemi, S., & Basaknejad, S. (2011). Investigating the effect of Islamic multifaceted treatment on students' depression and self-esteem. *Psychology and Religion*, 4(3), 31–48. [In Persian]

Mesbah, A. (2011). Analysis of the Concept of Spirituality and the Issue of Meaning. *Medical Ethics Journal*, 5(14), 23–39. [In Persian]

Mertens, D. M. (2008). Mixed Methods and the Politics of Human Research. In V. P. Clark, & J. W. Creswell (eds), *The Mixed Methods Reader*. California: Sage.

Mohammadi, S., Kajbaf, M., & Abedi, M. (2014). Investigating the effectiveness of monotheistic integrated therapy on the level of aggression in Qom prisoners. *Psychology and Religion*, 7(3), 47–64. [In Persian]

Myers, D. G. (2007). *Psychology* (8th ed.). New York: Worth Publishers.

Narouei-Nosrati, R., & Mansour, M. (2009). Personality formation, mental health and treatment of psychological disorders based on religious self-fulfillment theory. *Psychology and Religion*, 2(2), 7–40. [In Persian]

Nelson, J. M (2009). *Psychology, Religion, and Spirituality*. New York: Springer.

Numbers, R. (2003). Science without God: Natural laws and Christian beliefs. In D. Lindberg, & R. Numbers (Eds.), *When science and Christianity meet* (pp. 265–285). Chicago: University of Chicago Press.

Parhizkar, G. (2010). The Distinction or Sameness of Rūḥ and Nafs in the Quran. *Naqd Va Nazar*, 15(60), 125–145. [In Persian]

Patton, M. Q. (2002). *Qualitative research and evaluation methods* (3rd ed.). SAGE.

Patton, M. Q. (1990). *Qualitative evaluation and research methods* (2nd ed.). Newbury Park, CA: Sage.

Pourseyyed-Aghaei, Z. (2010). Investigation into God's Trust and Consent Religious Concepts Education Efficacy in Group Mode on Decrease of Tehran Region No 9. High School Girl's Anxiety. *Journal of Islamic Education*, 5(10), 79–100. [In Persian]

Qorbani-Vanajemi, M., Zandi, S., Nosrati, F., & Ghobari-Bonab, B. (2019). Mechanisms involved in the effectiveness of holy name repetition on stress reduction. *Clinical Excellence*, 9(1), 1–15. http://ce.mazums.ac.ir/article-1-444-en.html. [In Persian]

Quran. Translated by M. Fouladvand. Tehran: Islamic History and Education Studies Office. [In Persian]

Richards, P. S., & Bergin, A. E. (2005). *A Spiritual Strategy for Counseling and Psychotherapy* (2nd ed.). Washington, DC: American Psychological Association.

Roshan-Chesly, R., Shaeeri, M., Atrifard, M., Nikkhah, A., GhaemMaghami, B., & Rahimierad A. (2006). Investigating Psychometric Properties of "NEO-Five Factor Inventory" (NEO-FFI). *Clinical Psychology & Personality*, 1(16), 27–36. [In Persian]

Sahin, A. (2013). Reflections on the Possibility of an Islamic Psychology. *Archive for the Psychology of Religion*, 35(3), 321–335. https://doi.org/10.1163/15736121-12341270.

Santrock, J. W. (2018). *Psychology*. Translated by M. Firouzbakht. Tehran: Rasa. [In Persian]

Schultz, D., & Schultz, S. E. (2017). *Theories of Personality*. Translated by Y. Seyyed-mohammadi. Tehran: Virayesh. [In Persian]

Shaker, M., Sobhani, M. (2016). The Semantics of Soul in the Holy Qur'an. *Quran and Hadith Studies*, 9(1), 165–191. [In Persian]

Sharifi, M., Ahmadi, S., & Fatehizadeh, M. (2013). The impact of "behavioral – cognitive bereavement care in Islamic view" on "general health of the bereaved family". *Studies in Islam and Psychology, 7*(12), 113–134. http://islamicpsy.rihu.ac.ir/article_907.html?lang=en.

Sharifinia, M. (2008). A study of effectiveness of monotheistic integrated therapy in reduction of prisoners' delinquencies. *Studies in Islam and Psychology, 2*(2), 7–32. [In Persian]

Shojaei, M., Janbozorgi, M., Asgari, A., Gharavirad, S., Pasandideh, A. (2014). Classification Patterns of Personality Attributes in the Islamic Sources. *Studies in Islam and Psychology, 8*(14), 7–31. [In Persian]

Skinner, R. (1989). *Traditions, paradigms, and basic concepts in Islamic psychology* [Conference session]. Theory and Practice of Islamic Psychology, London, England.

Slife, B. D., Mitchell, L. J., & Whoolery, M. (2004). A theistic approach to therapeutic community: Non-naturalism and the Alldredge Academy. In P. S. Richards & A. E. Bergin (Eds.), *Casebook for a spiritual strategy for counseling and psychotherapy*. Washington, DC: American Psychological Association.

Tabatabaei, M. (1975). *Shiite Spirituality and 22 other articles*. Qom: Shiite Publication. [In Persian]

Tabatabaei, M. (1984). *Tafsir al-Mizan*. Translated by M. Mosavi-Hamedani. Qom: Islamic Publications Office. [In Persian]

Tashakkori, A., & Teddlie, C. (1998). *Mixed methodology: Combining qualitative and quantitative approaches*. Sage Publications.

Tavana, M. (2015). The Paradigm of Critical Realism: Approach to an Interdisciplinary Methodology. *Interdisciplinary Studies in the Humanities, 7*(1), 27–56. [In Persian]

Zandi, S., Shahabinejad, Z., & Borhan, A. (2017). Predicting defense mechanisms based on big five personality traits among university students. *Zanko Journal of Medical Sciences, 56*, 21–32. http://zanko.muk.ac.ir/article-1-166-en.html. [In Persian]

Zandi, S., Rahimi, A., & Mousavi-Nasl, M. (2021). Consequences of death awareness in adolescents' lives: A qualitative study. *Journal of Counseling Research, 19*(76), 209–233. http://irancounseling.ir/journal/article-1-1441-en.html. [In Persian]

Zibakalam, F. (2007). *The Philosophical Thought in the West*. Tehran: University of Tehran Press. [In Persian]

Printed in the United States
by Baker & Taylor Publisher Services